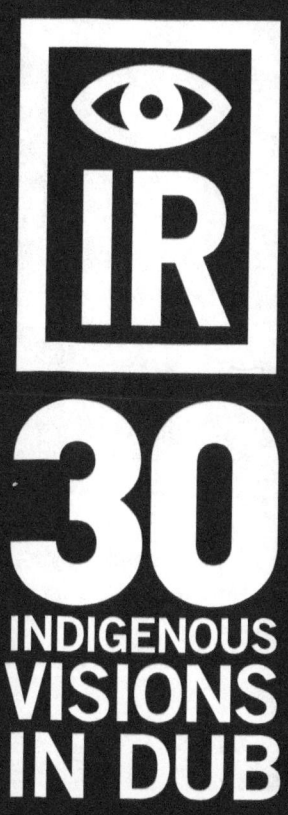

IR
30
INDIGENOUS VISIONS IN DUB

IR 30

DESIGN, BOOK LAYOUT AND ARTWORK....**Dubdem**

PROOFREADING....**Jahteecha, Mapuchedub**

WEBOLOGY,E BOOK LOGISTICS....**Tapedave**

EDITOR....**The Ghost**

PHOTOGRAPHS....**Ramjac, Mapuchedub, Dubdem & Fabdub**

DUB LOGISTICS....**Senor Açai and many who are in the shadows**

PUBLISHED BY TFTT | 2012
TORONTO, CANADA, SOLOMON ISLANDS, WALKIR VERGANI (BRASIL).
ISBN 978-1-927801-03-1

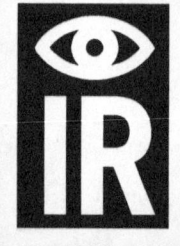

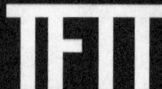

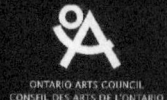

INDIGENOUS VISIONS IN DUB

05	IR9: INDIGENOUS AND BLACK WISDUBS
64	THE VISUAL REVOLUTION MIX 1
78	IR1
88	THIS DUB IS FOR GALDINO
96	BLAKK INDIAN RESISTANCE
114	EXPLORING SPIRITUAL CONNECTIONS
134	A BRASILIAN EXPERIENCE
144	THE VISUAL REVOLUTION MIX 2

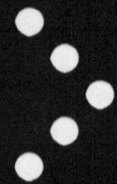

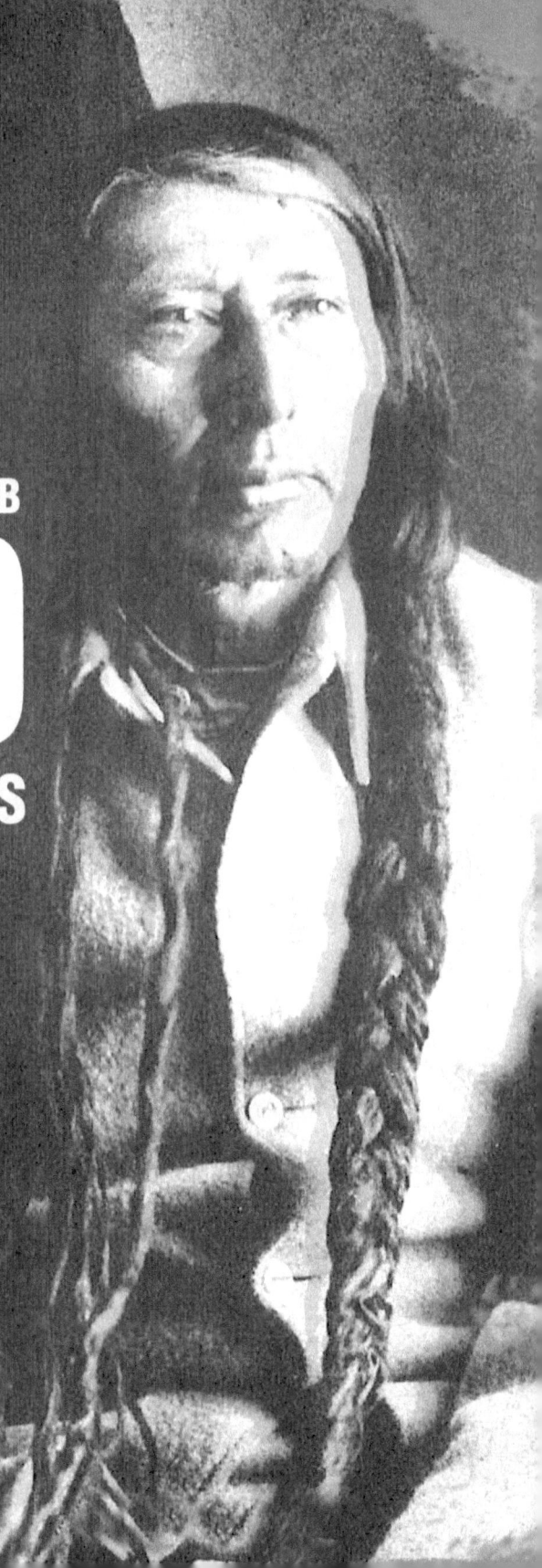

ATUADUB
IR9
INDIGENOUS AND BLACK WISDUBS

IR9
INDIGENOUS AND BLACK WISDUBS

Indigenous and
Black Philosophy
& Political Thought

By Atua Dub

Visual dub mixes
by Dubdem

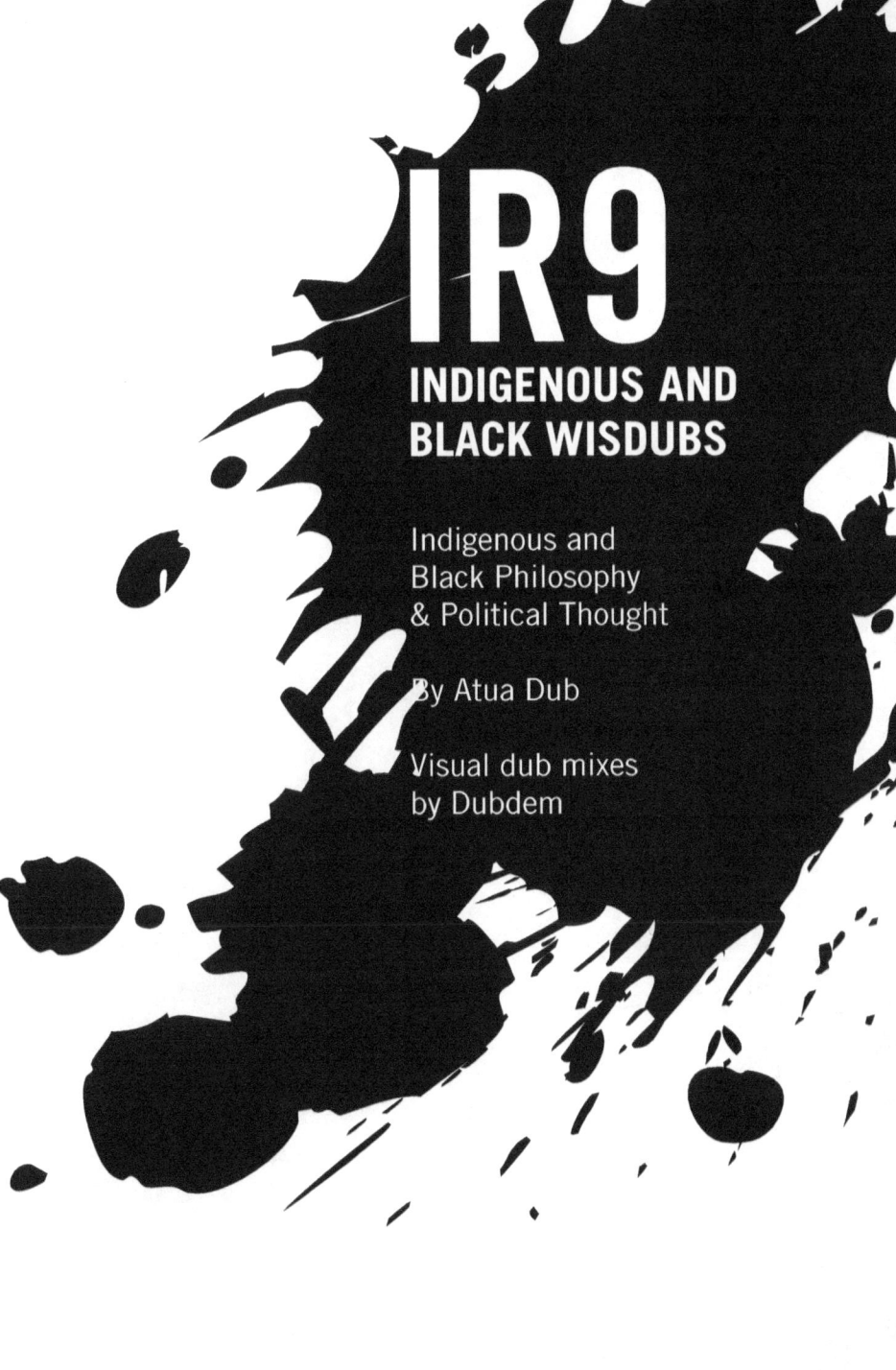

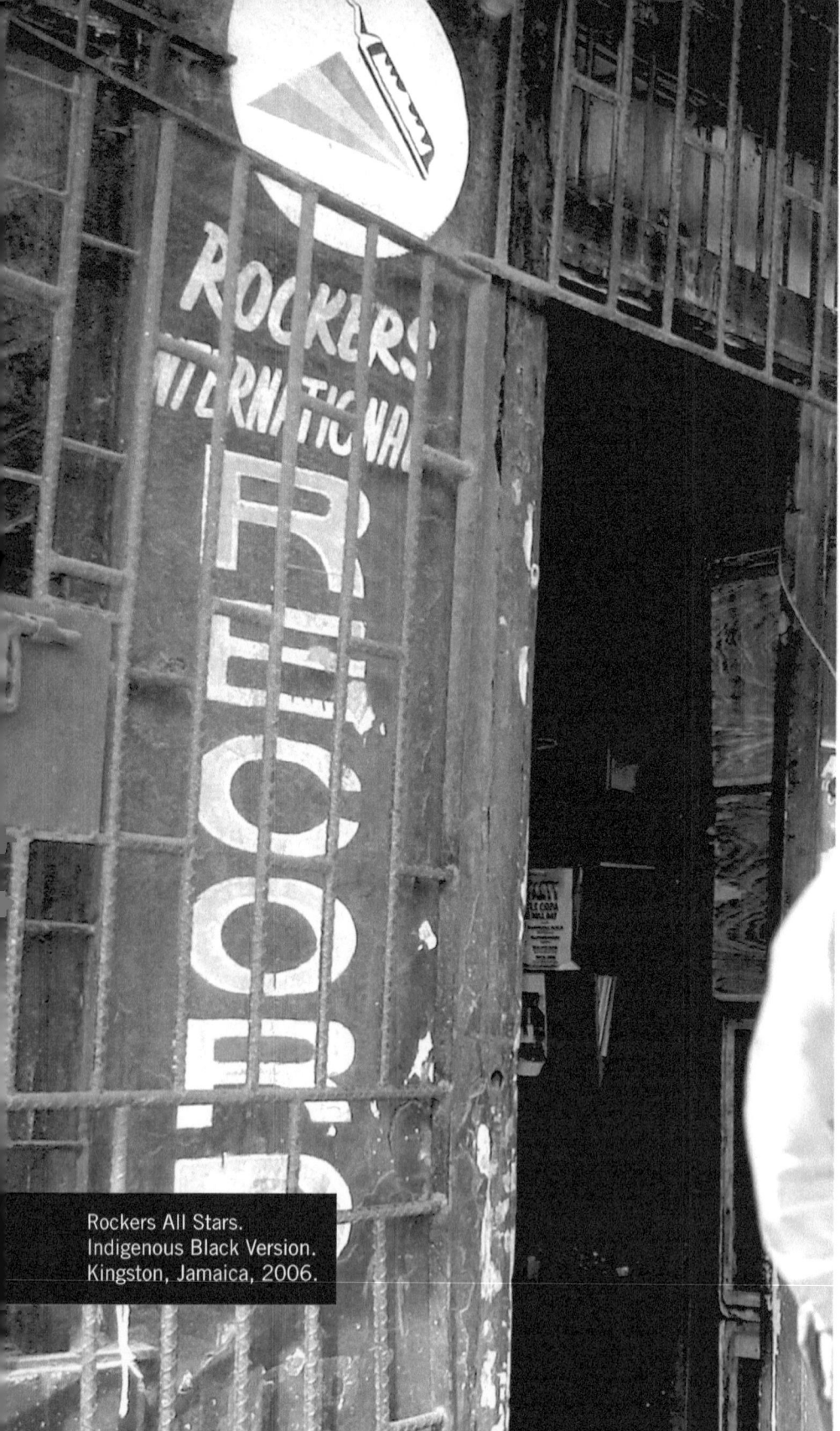

Rockers All Stars.
Indigenous Black Version.
Kingston, Jamaica, 2006.

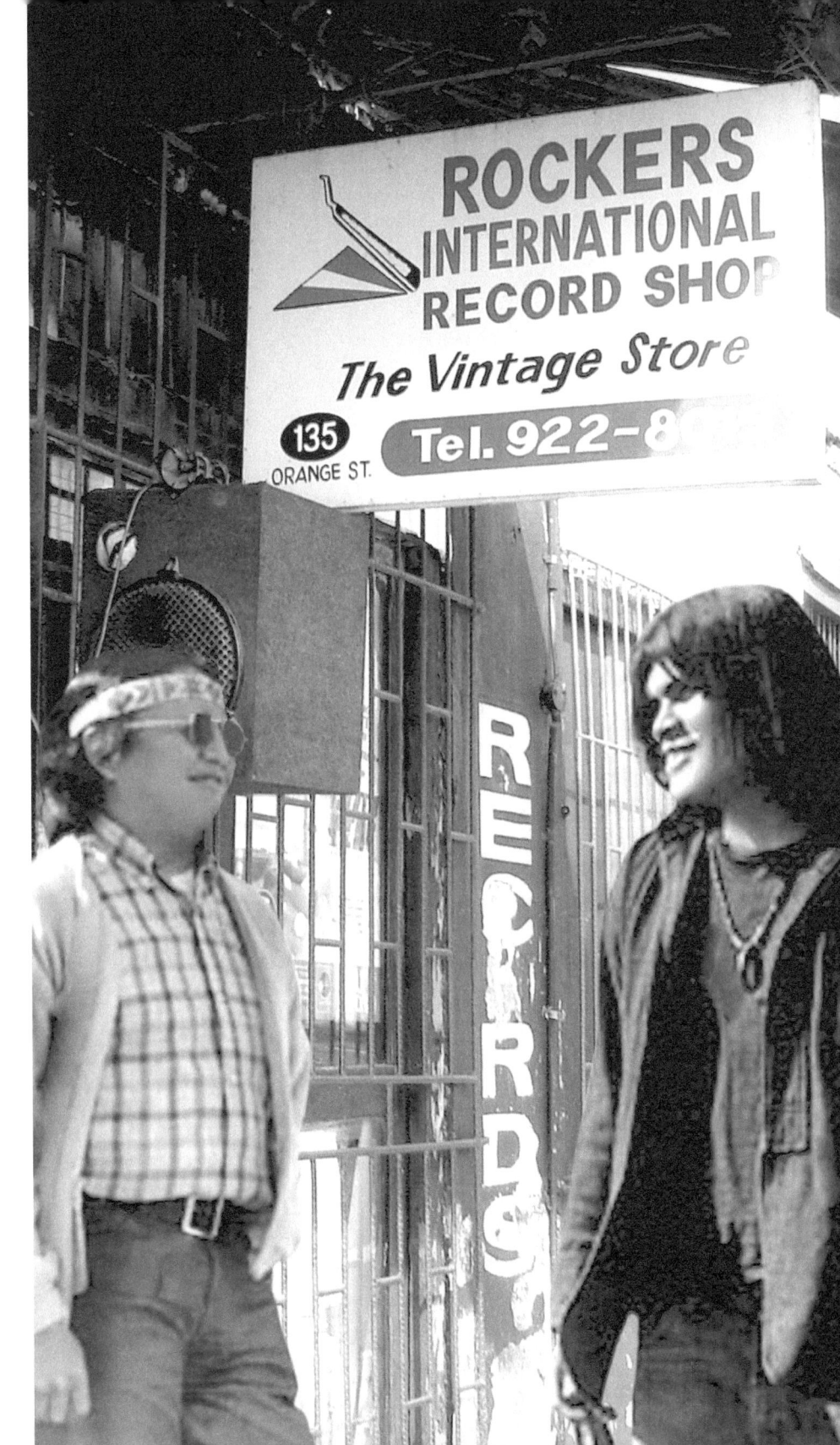

Copyright 2005 by Atua dub. All rights reserved.

ISBN

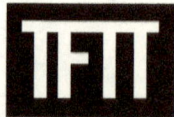

TFTT The Fire This Time Pub. Toronto, Sosolakam.

Credits:
Front cover, graphic design by Dubdem.

The cover of this book shows the famed resistance leader Poundmaker an indigenous warrior with great spiritual power who also had long dreadlocks. He served as the inspiration for The Fire This Time track "Poundmakers Dub".

Photos on pages 2 and 38: images from Jamaica by Dubdem, images of indigenous people by Ilka Hartmman.

Copy editor, text layout: Mapuchedub.
Photo on page 53: Dandara Dub.

This is an autonomous TFTT / IR (Indigenous Resistance) production to access other TFTT / IR productions i.e. free vinyl,
Kona Warrior comics, videos visit www.firethistime.com
Email us at tftt3000@yahoo.ca

We take this opportunity to salute Leonard Peltier, Mumia Abu Jamal & all political prisoners as well as the good folk of D.C.C.N and Sosolakam where this book was written.

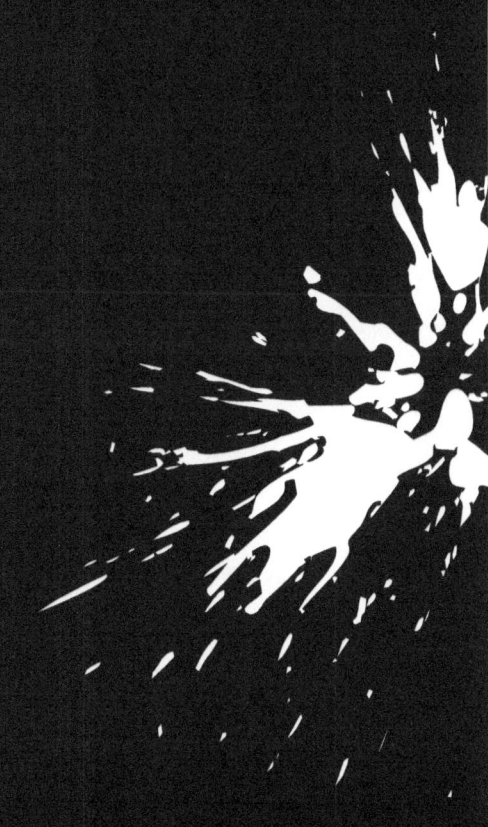

THE MIXING BOARD

14 Track One: **Bass**

18 Track Two: **Drums**

20 Track Three: **John Trudell**

30 Track Four: **Jean "Binta" Breeze**

32 Track Five: **Douglas Cardinal**

36 Track Six: **Jeannette Armstrong**

38 Track Seven: **Tohununo, Pesio, Atua Dub**

46 Track Eight: **Douglas Cardinal, Jeannette Armstrong, Atua Dub**

50 Track Nine: **Assata Shakur, Douglas Cardinal and Jeannette Armstrong, Atua Dub**

Track One
Bass

Dreams and their significance have paramount importance in many cultures especially indigenous ones.

Dreams provided some of the crucial basslines for this and other dub recordings. Years ago we were visiting a sacred valley in Zimbabwe, a place known for its ancient monuments. We spent the night there, sleeping in a circular structure. That night in a dream we saw very clearly the cover and various pages of a book of Native philosophy. Two years later we were visiting Jeannette Armstrong in the Okanagan valley where she lives and she commented to us that she wanted to show us a project she had just completed. She took out a book, it was entitled "The Native Creative Process" it was a writing collaboration between herself and Douglas Cardinal with photographs by Greg Young Ing it was among other things, a discussion of indigenous philosophy and was released by the indigenous owned and operated press Theytus Books.

When we looked at it, we were astounded because it was exactly the book we saw in our dream in Zimbabwe. A few years later we were in Kingston, Jamaica preparing to record the cd "Dancing on John Wayne's Head" with dub maestro Augustus Pablo, when we had an incredible dream. In this dream we took some of the indigenous philosophy present in "The Native Creative Process" and put it into dub tracks. The dream showed us the importance of making this philosophy more widely available in order to enrich people's lives. The Fire This Time created various musical tracks where we inserted this philosophy into dub tracks.

When we travelled to Havana, Cuba to collaborate with fugitive Black Panther Assata Shakur we took with us a copy of "The Native Creative Process" and we discussed the book with Assata Shakur. Some of our reflections inspired other dub tracks.

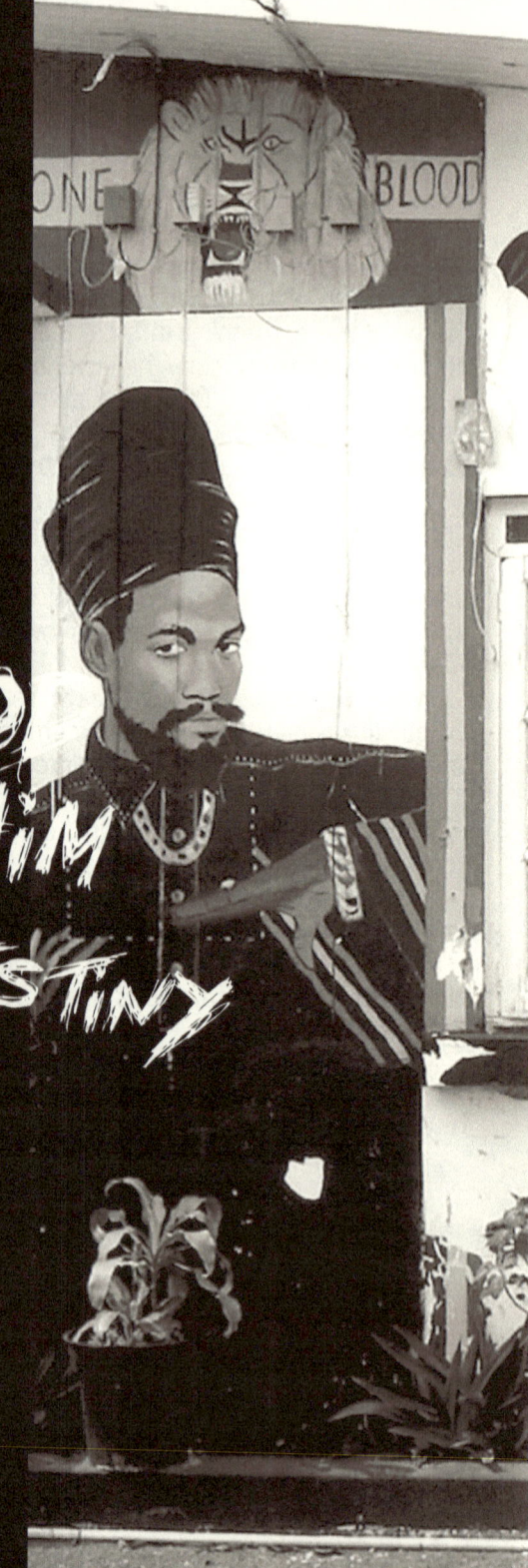

One Blood, One Aim, One Destiny

Junior Reid's One Blood Records. Kingston, Jamaica, 2006.

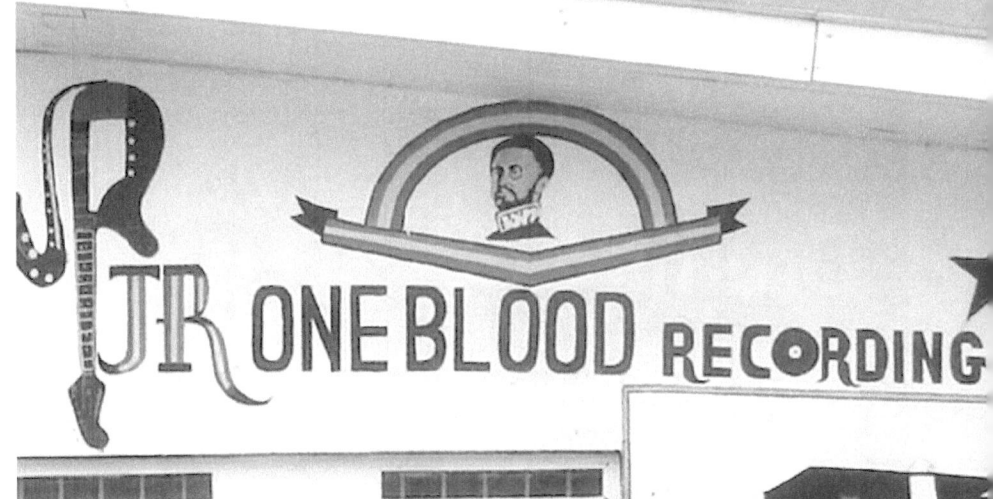

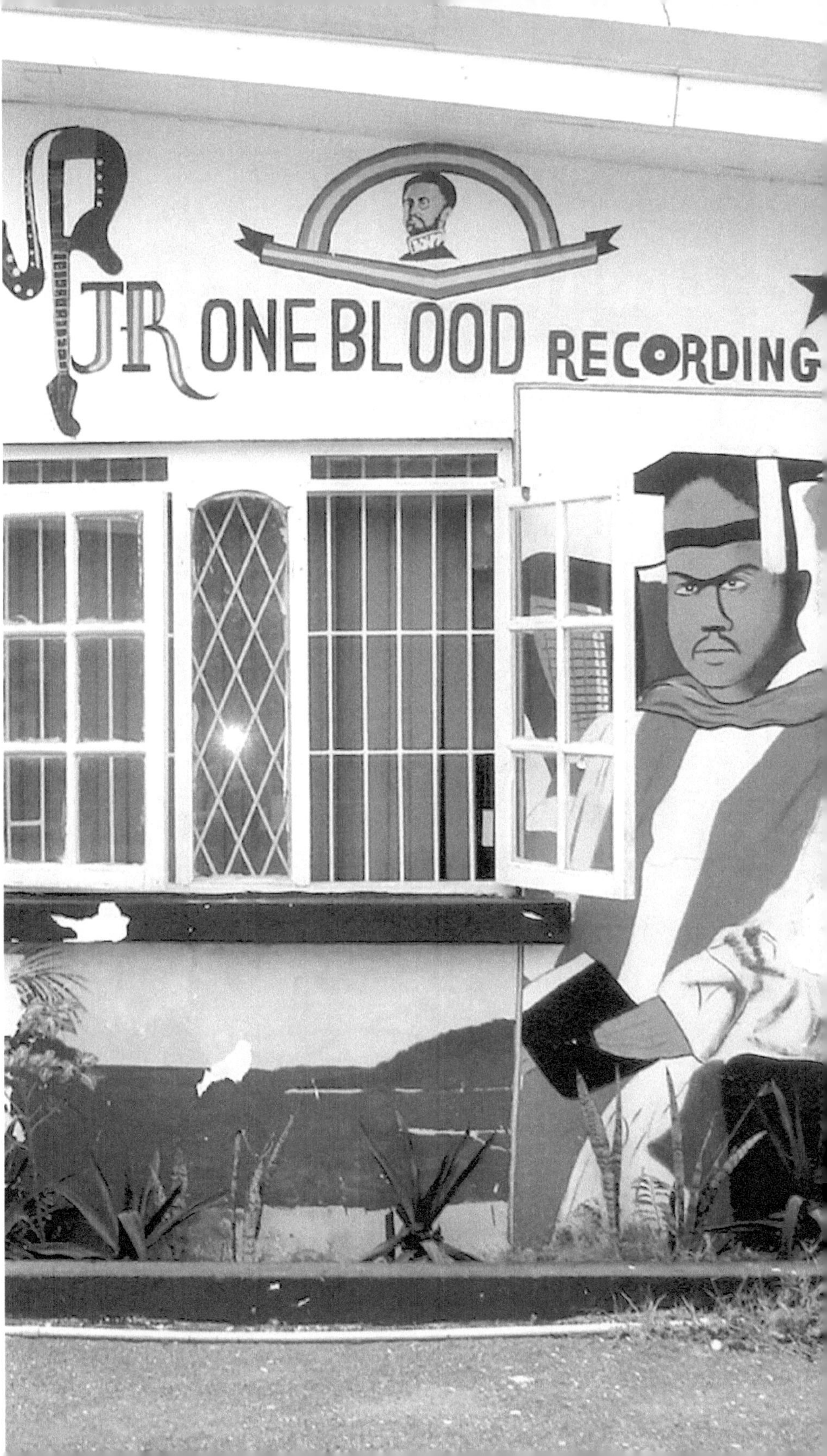

Track Two
Drums

The fluid combination of drum and bass is crucial to creating the rhythm that drives many a reggae and dub track. In the dub tracks we create sometimes we will focus on one drum rimshot, isolate it in the mix and throw a lot of echo and reverb on it.

At other moments you will hear a drum rimshot followed by total silence. One gets to hear the drum /indigenous wisdub/wisdom in a unique way.

Like many indigenous cultures dub music values the quiet moments. Moments of silence. As a friend of ours George from the Solomon Islands commented to us:

"What is not said in Melanesian communities is often more important than what is said"

We thought this was a very dub comment.

Someone once remarked after listening to a piece of dub music that the track felt incomplete, something was missing.

However realizing that they were accustomed to listening to music that followed more conventional forms, we suggested to them to go back and listen to the tracks again and to try and really listen for all the subtleties in between the moments of silences. A couple of days later, they returned very animated; pointing out to us all the new things they were able to pick out.

This book is meant to be like tracks of dub music where the drum/wisdub keeps echoing and the reverb though quiet keeps going and going and where repeated listening reveals hidden frequencies.

Enjoy this dub mix
Atua Dub Selectah /Mixing Engineer/ Producer

Track Three
John Trudell

> •••• Former chairperson of the American Indian Movement John Trudell was described by the F.B.I as being one of the most dangerous men in America solely because of the power of his oratory.

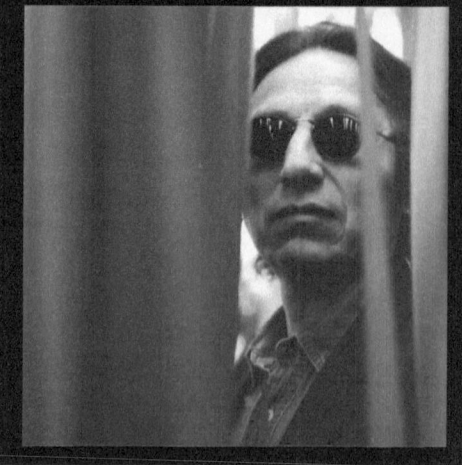

Leaders know you
Can't trust one
who follows

Followers know
Not to trust
one who leads

It's like control
It's a mistake to
try and be in control
Influence
Influence
the best you can

use your mind as clearly as possible to influence what is happening

Now why would I want to save democracy
just plain and simple realities
why would I want to save what is essentially
a nazi outfit and nazi operation to my people
democracy did what the Nazis did to the Jews
this is no name calling
this is the reality
so why would I as an indigenous person
a tribal person
want to save democracy
make it

better

Now if you were black, democracy told me that I was property
and when they got off that, they just continued
to treat me as if I was property
and imply to me that I am inferior
so if I am black
why am I concerned about saving democracy
if I am woman
democracy is based on the principle
that I have no say

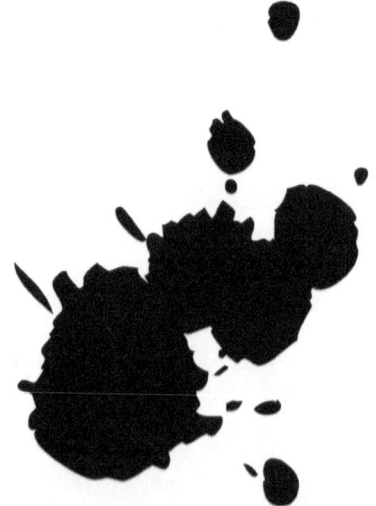

They say whoever has the most
money
has the most power

that's not true
whoever makes the most money
basically is

greedy

They say whoever controls
the political vote system
that's power
no that's not power
That's exploitation and deceit

But if we believe that these things are
power then obviously we don't know ourselves
and we don't trust ourselves enough
to know that we are connected
to the real power source
which is life and earth

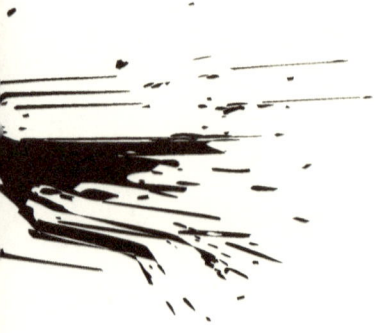

We live in a political society
      where they have all the power
      by their definition of power
      but they fear people who go
      out and speak the truth
      that's why they spy on political
      organizations
      that's why they spy on themselves
      they say we are paranoid.

I am paranoid

      because I don't trust them.
      They have never given me one
      instance when they could be trusted.
      They are afraid we are going to
      use our minds
      use our minds to seek clarity.

**Motive intention behavior
these things must be in sync**

**our motives must be in sync
with our intentions**

our motives must be in sync
with our behavior.

Isolation

kindling separated from the spark

We have been deliberately programmed
with the wrong conception of what the value of worth
is really about.

You have to understand the intensity of the attack.
The respectability and legitimacy of the attack.

From the time most of us were children, television was there to
tell us other children would like us better if we bought these
things. And we have not escaped it. Now they say
buy these kinds of cars
this kind of deodorant
this kind of underwear
It's advertising for the human
but it's also an assault against our spiritual integrity.

That we will be better the more we consume
it's like junk
it creates a need
be aware
your minds are being drugged
it's the material junkies.

It's the hope and promise that things will get
better.
But generally in most minds, things will get better relates to
material rewards.

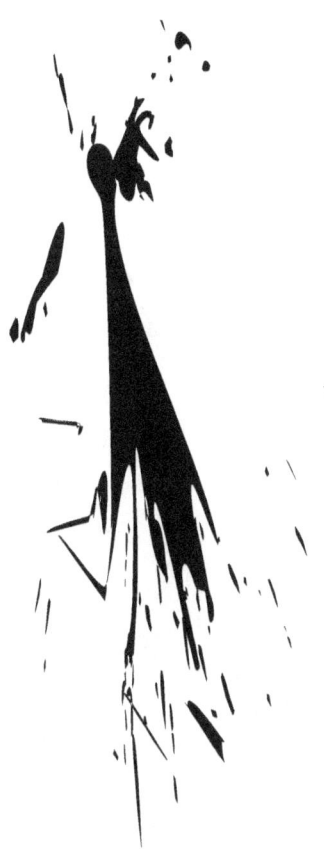

We worked your jobs
still we are poor
we die in your wars
and you make more wars
we obeyed your laws
still we are not safe
we gave you a chance
and still you don't trust us
we wanted to get along
still we are wanted
we heard what you said
still you are talking
we drank from your well
still we are thirsty

Rod Taylor's Lonely Girl.

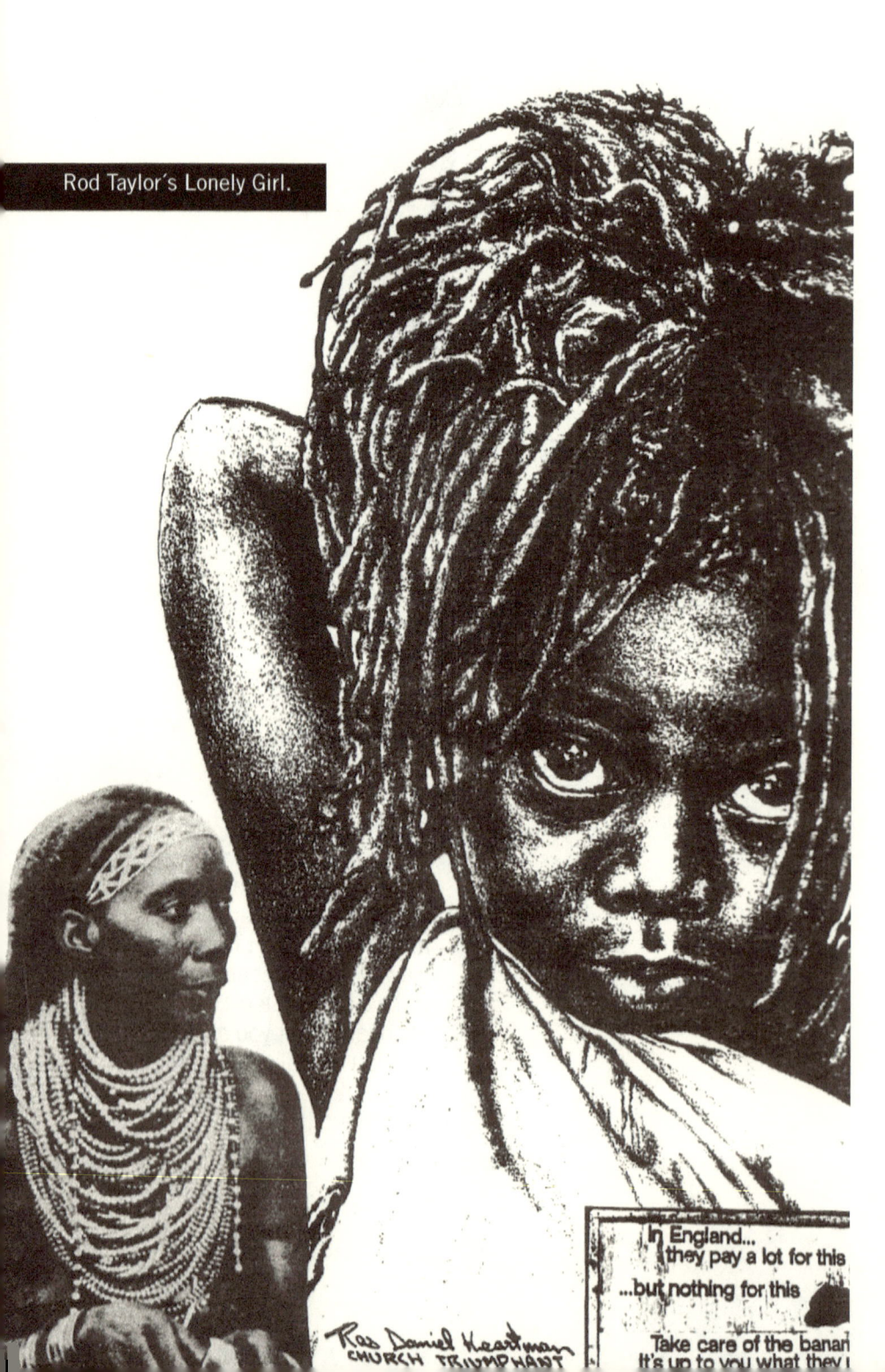

In England...
they pay a lot for this
...but nothing for this
Take care of the banan
It's up to you what they

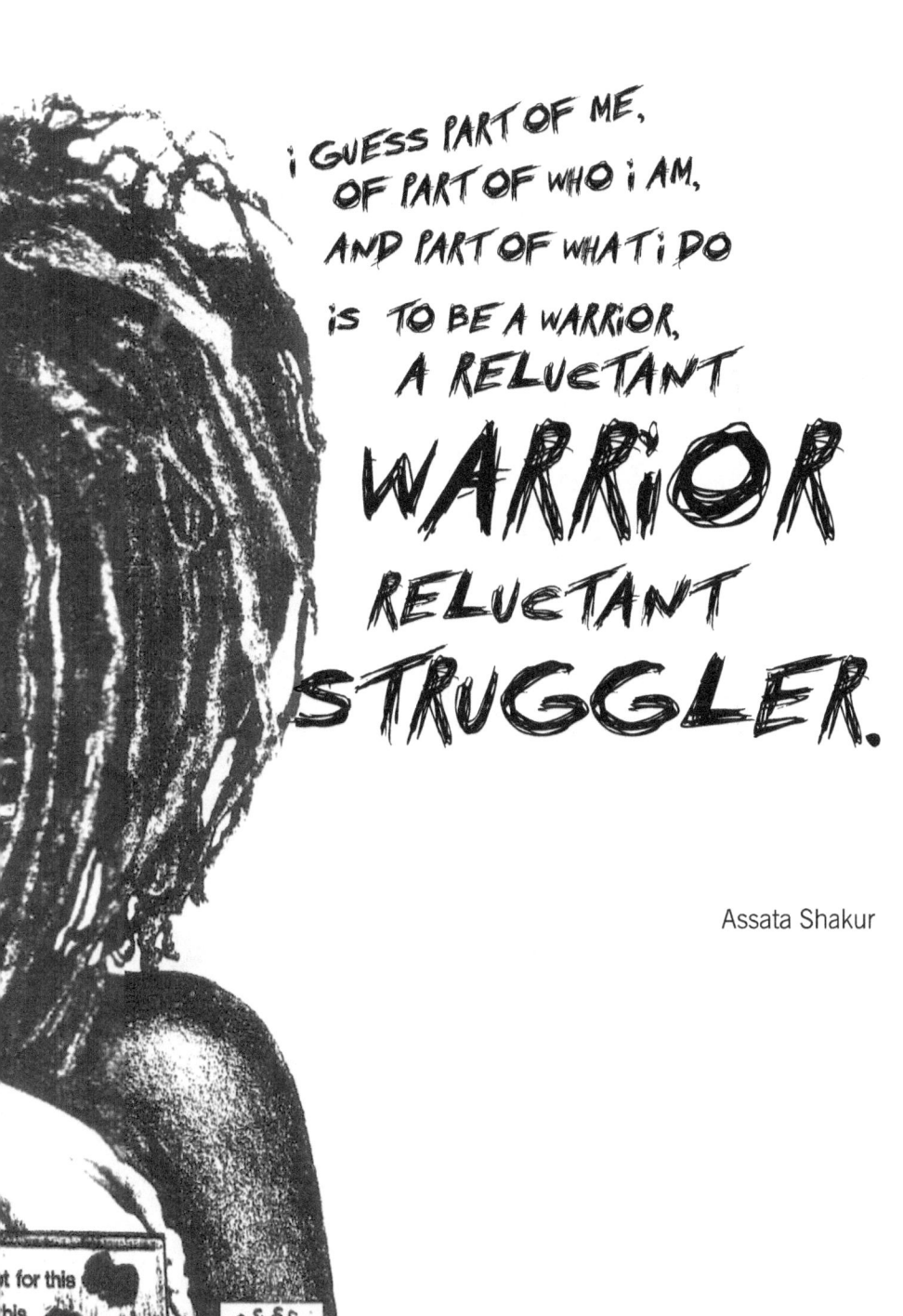

Track Four
Jean Binta Breeze

• • •
• • Born in Jamaica with Arawak Indian blood,
Breeze is a visionary & acclaimed writer;
dub poet, and theatrical performer.

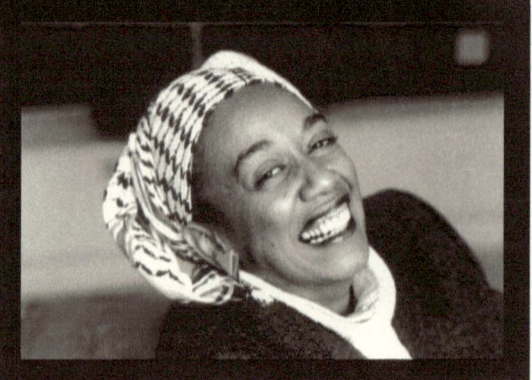

On any land that makes up this planet called Earth, there were people that were put there by the Creator and who by the very fact that they were the first people of the land share an understanding of that land, how to tread on that land, how to live on that land without destroying it. How to love that land as something given to one to take care of. So I think that whoever we are, where we come from, when we are on somebody's land, we want to make contact in an extremely humble way with the Native people that the Creator has blessed with knowledge of that land. Part of our problem is that often when we go onto other people's land we walk with such arrogance. Sometimes we bring with us a mentality that says because we have certain things we have more power and we misinterpret the humility of the people who know and love that land.

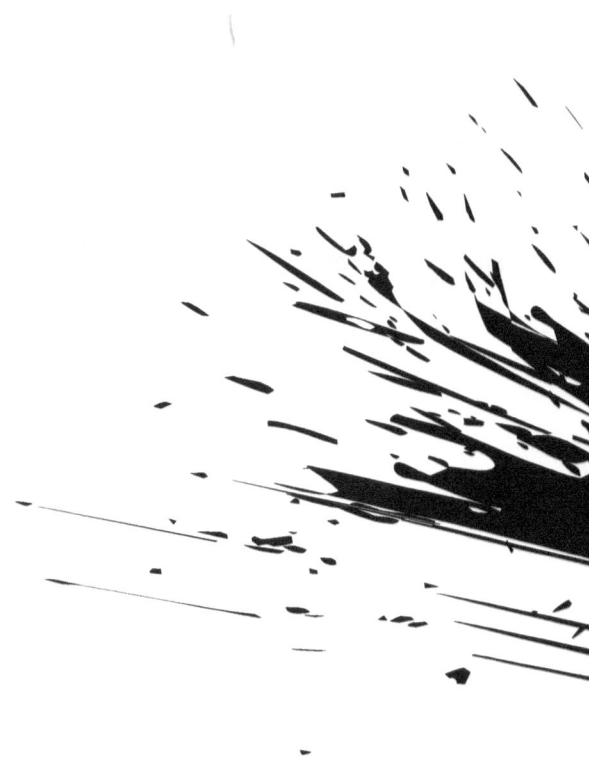

Track Five
Douglas Cardinal

> A Métis pipe carrier and renown architect, Douglas Cardinal was responsible for the design of the Museum Of Civilization located in Hull, Canada.

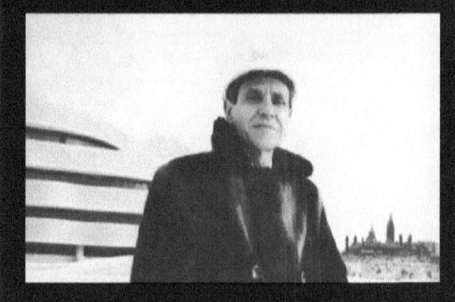

So it's almost like a barometer, the more upset they are getting you must be doing something right, you must be achieving something. People think that when they achieve things that everybody is going to come and applaud them, they don't realize that when you are achieving things that's when everybody is really upset because you are shaking up their lives, you are making them think, you are making them uncomfortable with what is known. So if you expect any rewards in that way for changing things you aren't going to get it. No one appreciates you changing anything, there's too much invested in the status quo. You have to be a warrior in that sense of realizing that you will get all sorts of adversities.

Well I think the whole way of looking at women is wrong. We don't look at women as people with minds, as people that have a great deal to contribute. Women as partner. Our society looks at women more or less as objects, sex objects, as mothers, as nurturers. Its changing quite a bit now, there are more doors open to them but still there is a great deal of sexism. Men feel intimidated in the work place with women as bosses or equals. One has to state that all the premises that men have of women are basically wrong and you start from there. Even the language is wrong. The whole way of languaging, the way we speak comes from a paternalistic, judeo christian religion, that is entrenched in our language.

> **WE ALMOST HAVE TO RECREATE A NEW LANGUAGE WHICH SHOWS RESPECT FOR WOMEN. I THINK AS MEN IF WE WALKED IN WOMEN'S SHOES FOR A WHILE WE WOULD BE OUTRAGED.**

The way one is cultured, programmed as a man makes it really hard to go over and really walk in the shoes of a woman and understand the difficulties living in this society they have. The whole built environment has no relationship to women and children. It is hard power, its ego, its phallic. But there's nothing that is nurturing or empathetic about our built environment. Our cities are physical manifestations of where we are at. Women and children do not belong in our cities. Just a bunch of power tripping men belong in our cities. They are not fit places to develop and grow. Apartments aren't designed for women and children. Its almost as if that they are force to live in alien surroundings in order to survive.

I think we have a responsibility to get over there with the women and to walk with them, we have the responsibility to understand where they are coming from, to listen and to respond to them. And it's hard sometimes because they have also been programmed by men to be our reflection instead of themselves. But when women speak out that have an understanding of who they are as women and what their contributions is, we should listen and support them, rather than domineer and annihilate them and it should be our task to learn from them.

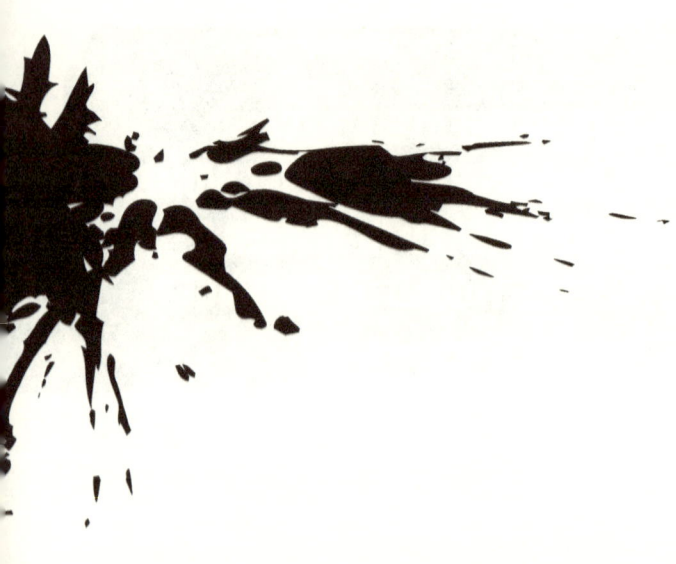

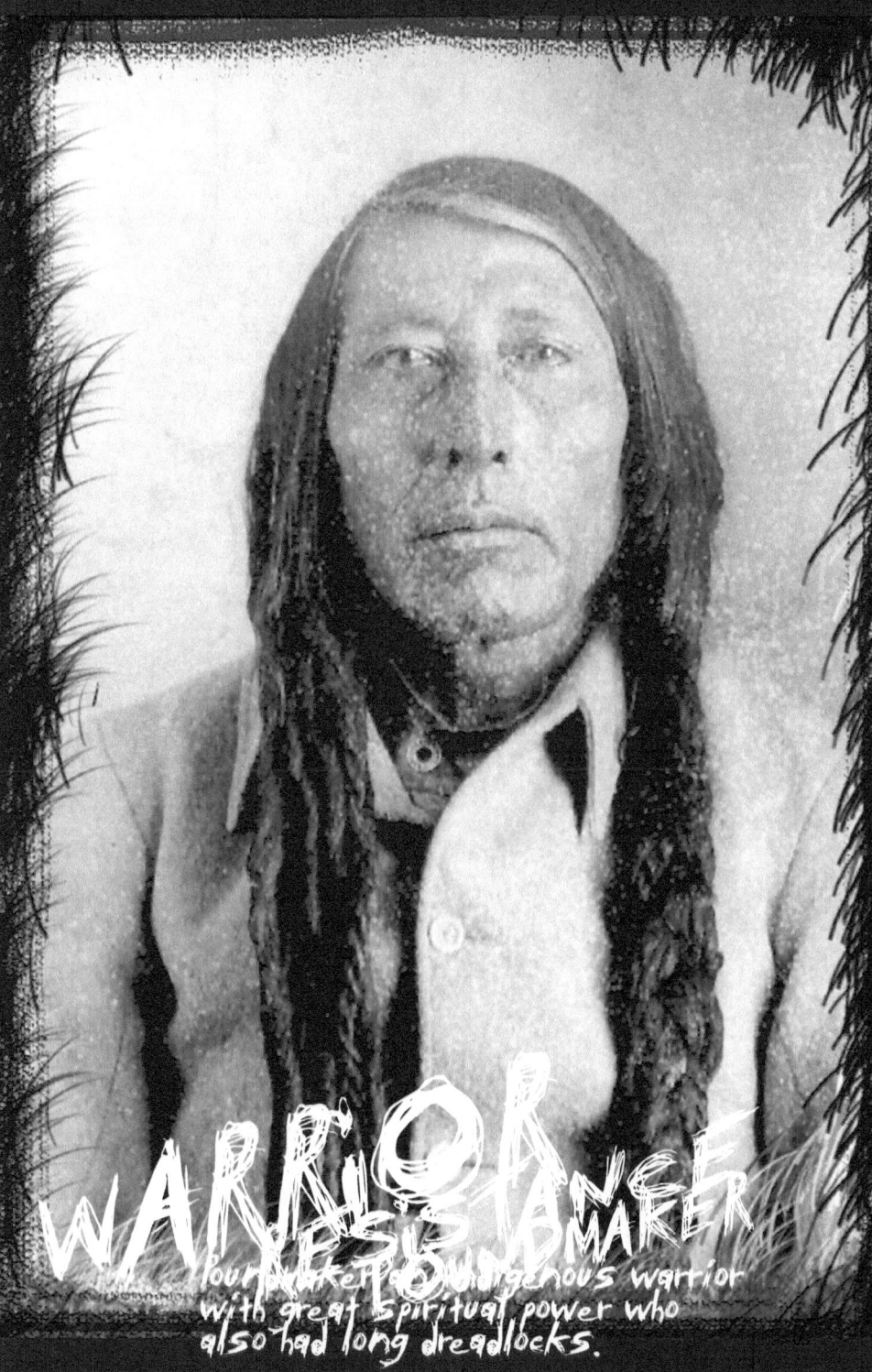

WARRIOR YES IS MAKER
Four Maker, an indigenous warrior with great spiritual power who also had long dreadlocks.

Track Six
Jeannette Armstrong

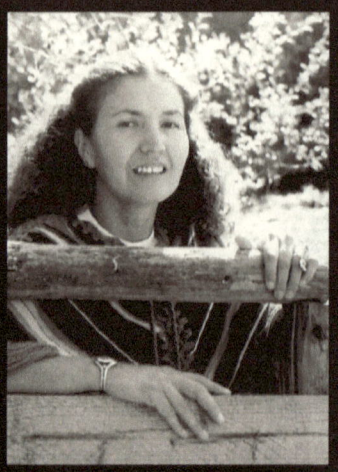

• • An Okanagan Indian writer, poet, educator,
•   sculptor, singer and author of the novels
     "Slash" and "Whispering in Shadows".

I got a clear message from my grandmother that no one has a right to coerce or own another person or act in a way which determines by force that the person doesn't have a choice.

No person
has that right over another person.

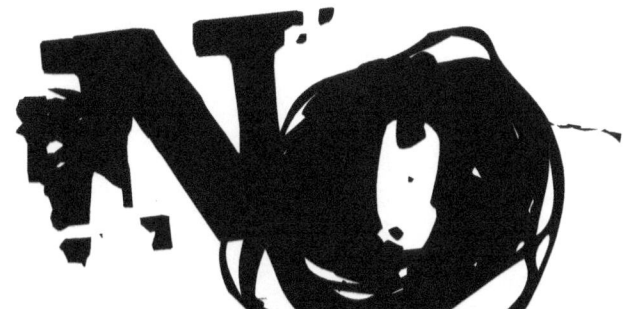

Track Seven
Tohununo, Pesio, Atua Dub

Tohununo and Pesio are indigenous musicians from the Solomon Islands in the Pacific.

The money world
is full of noise
people making noise
because they
are afraid of silence

in the silence
they will see

their guilt

In the sacred way
you see your meaning

they have to talk
because they are
afraid of silence
and in that noise they
make empty promises
that they aren't related to

when you are quiet
you are connected
your silence brings out
your understanding that
you are part of the sacred world
and your connection to it
It's the silence that connects you
to the sacred world

}

even before heavy rainfall
you can feel the presence of
something about to happen

there's a silence

the money world doesn't hear
this silence

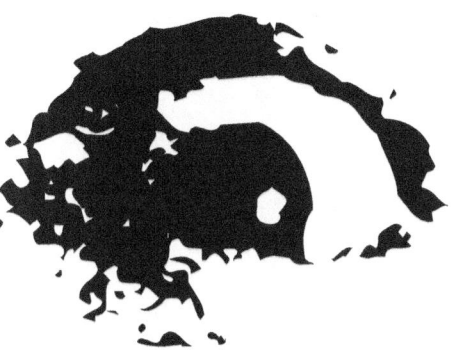

if you have doubt
about someone
wait and watch
because the more
you wait
the more the person will
reveal their true character

indigenous people were dependent
on survival skills
the emphasis was on using your
survival skills, knowledge and understandings
in order to be productive
in order to survive
whereas today people are busy
for the sake of being busy
It's often not about being productive }

in the indigenous world you are free
to move, free to be creative
you aren't bound, limited by material
possessions and at the same time
you have learnt survival skills
to survive in tough and trying times

in contrast if you remove
someone out of their familiar
context in the money world
they are hopeless
they need that money world
to make them stand

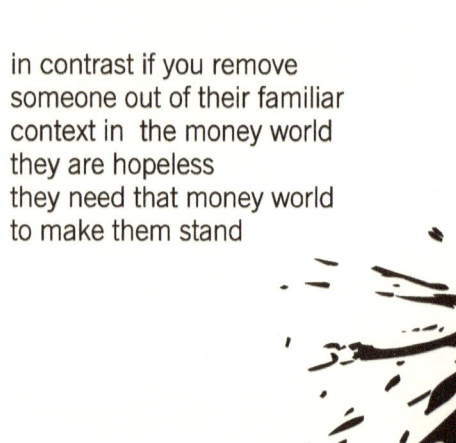

understand the concept of sacred things
learn that they are moments to hold things close
wait, wait for the right moment to reveal them
because they will carry with them a sacred power
learn learn to be quiet
there are moments to speak

moments to listen

in times of danger
be still

observe

the money world
this money world
is moving too fast
for people to take notice
of things
things that are important
this is the blindness that will defeat them
open your eyes to the concept of sacred things

in the ways of the sacred indigenous world
the people's eyes were open

they were encouraged not to concentrate on
accumulating material possessions
instead they were taught to accumulate a wide range of
survival skills, knowledge and understandings
they could take with them wherever they traveled and moved
these are the ways of the sacred indigenous world.

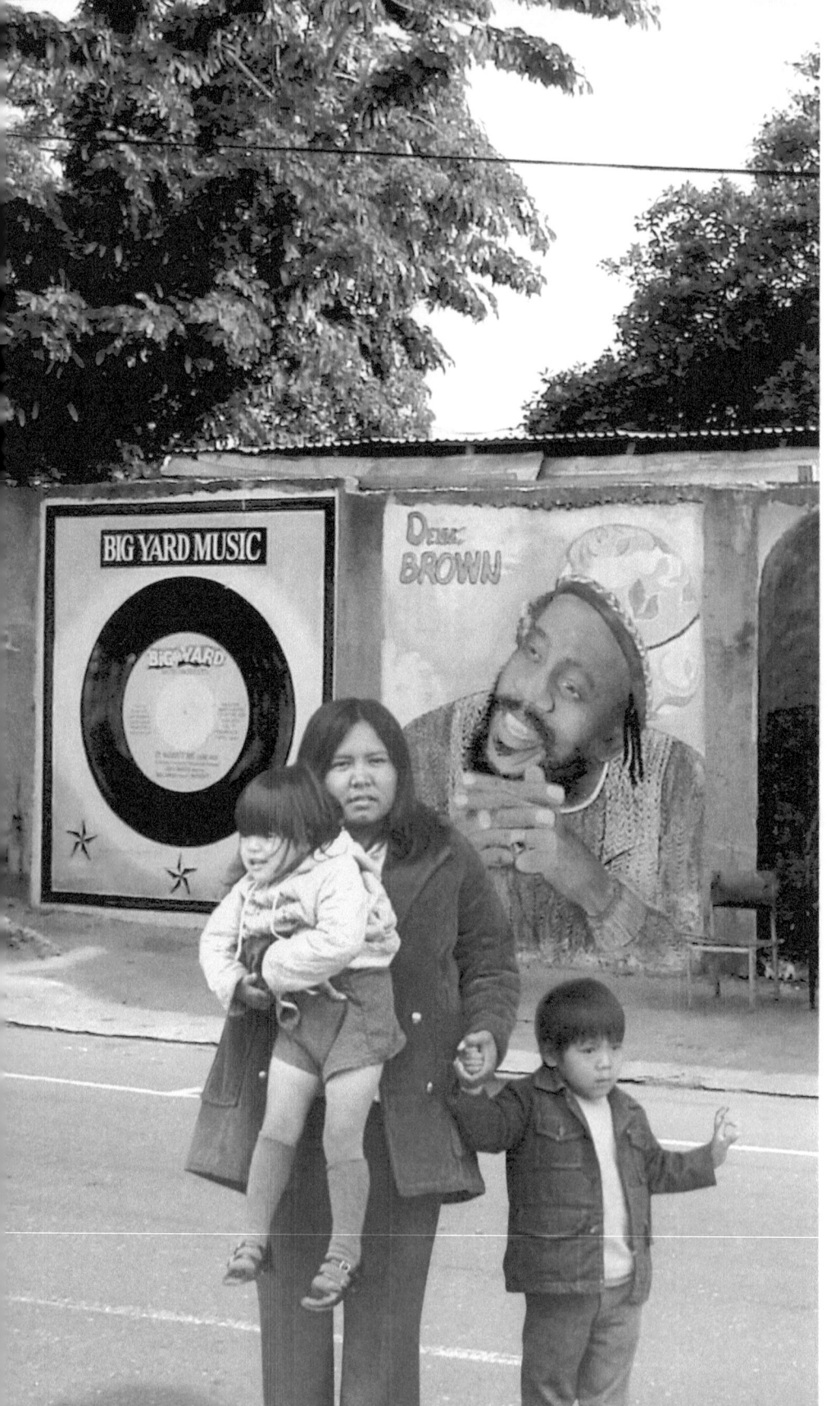

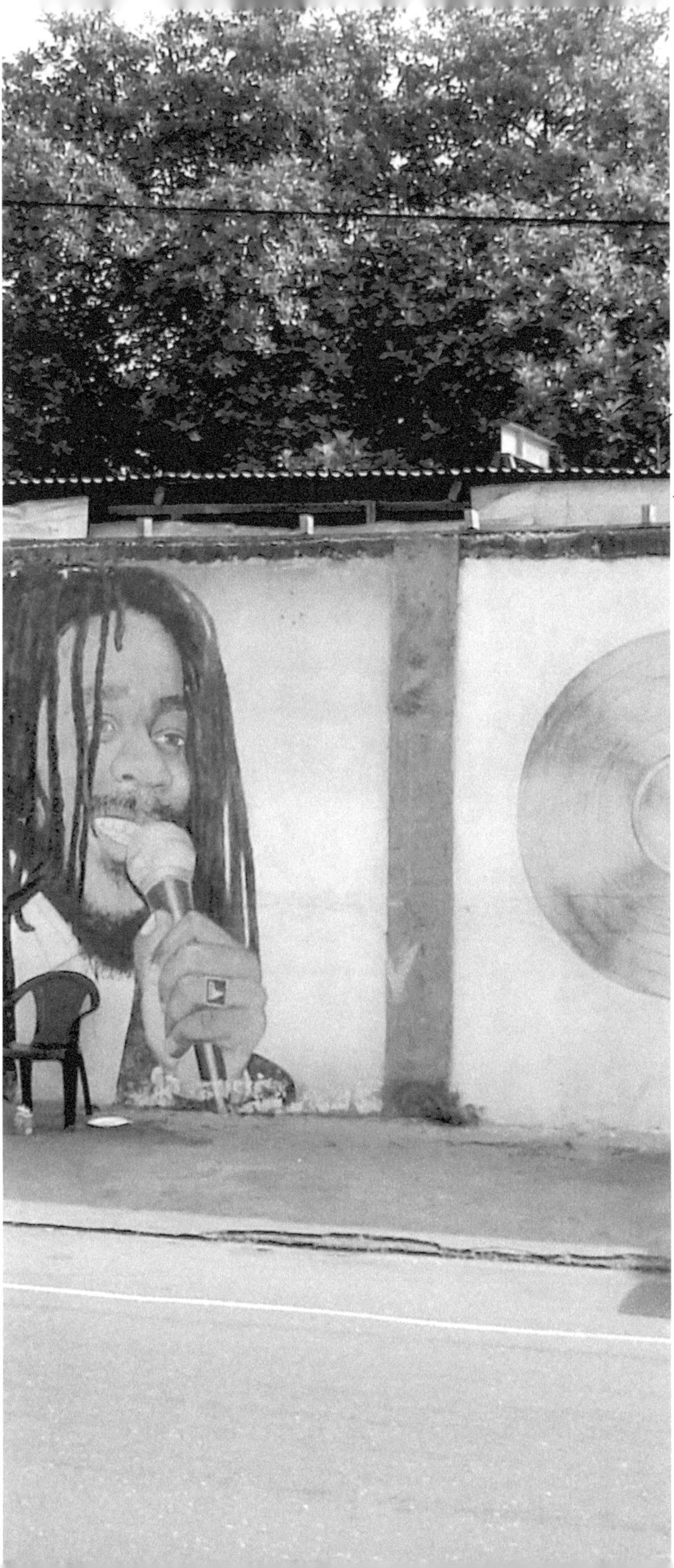

Indigeneous Black Dub Mix. Orange Street, Kingston, Jamaica, 2006.

Track Eight
Douglas Cardinal, Jeannette Armstrong, Atua Dub

In many languages in the Pacific the word Atua means "spirit" or "ghost".

D. Cardinal/J. Armstrong:

Here is the wisdom of our elders. As an individual you are both male and female. Men and women are very powerful working together. As a man if you allow yourself to be sourced by women, to be coached, to learn from, to take the contribution that they are, then partnership is very powerful. As an individual if you don't allow the female to emerge in you then you can only go so far. If you have soft power, if you have compassion, love then you can do anything.

Atua Dub:

Once I was driving in a car with the poet John Trudell he recited part of this poem to me:

when they first met
she couldn't forget
times only purpose
was for them to gather
they talked together
and were gentle
they laid together
and were aflame
she told him her dreams
trusting him with her prayers
she needed a friend
she needed a man
as newness stretches thin
it turns out he didn't understand
part of the man let her down
part of the man couldn't give
part of the man he never was
part of the man
part of her life
been through all of this before

}

For myself there's something incredibly sad about this poem because I imagine it reflects a situation that many women have gone through, that sense of disappointment that the potential partnership they dream about cannot take place because of the limitations of the man. As men we need to look deep within and approach this with great humility and from the point of view that we have so much to learn from women. Our lack of willingness to do so has been to the great detriment of our own potential as men but on a more important level it has resulted in a huge loss of potential for movements that struggle against Babylon system as Douglas Cardinal says together that partnership can be so incredibly powerful therefore imagine the inverse.

D. Cardinal/J. Armstrong:

I have learnt from native people that the most powerful force is soft power, caring and commitment together.

You need that center to make a contribution creatively. You need its power to realize your vision. You can have visions and dreaming but how you realize them depends on caring and commitment. Soft power is more powerful than adversarial or hard power because it is resilient. By its nature soft power is giving and flexible, it is woman power, its female power.

Atua dub:

One of the things that really struck me observing indigenous communities in turtle island was the presence and respect shown to the men in the communities who were gentle and soft in their approach. This had a profound impact on me because it presented an expanded alternative view of how a man can be. You see growing up in the Caribbean when someone called you "soft" it was said with a very negative connotation.

D. Cardinal/J. Armstrong:

You can't order the universe but you can find what natural forces are in it that you need in order to do things right. You must allow yourself to be comfortable with chaos and dependenton it to get things done.

Atua Dub:

"Control" one of the biggest illusions Babylon system tries to convince the public of. Men trying to control the women they are with in order to prove that they are a 'man" is just one example of this futility.

This type of futile thinking is inherent in the premise behind concepts like the police state. As John Trudell commented to me:

Control

It's a mistake to try and be in control
influence
influence
the best you can
use your mind as clearly as possible

but if you try and control
It's like trying to make a dam
there's damnation
right there"

Track Nine

Assata Shakur, Douglas Cardinal, Jeanette Armstrong, Atua Dub

 Black Panther Assata Shakur has contributed many years of radical activism and was imprisoned on false charges. She survived attempts by the USA government to murder her and escaped from a high security prison in Amerikkka. Currently Assata lives in Havana, Cuba. She is also the aunt of rapper Tupac Shakur.

D. Cardinal/J. Armstrong:

I have often spoken about being a warrior from the native perspective. Such a warrior operates from commitment and a way of being, a commitment to take a stand. A stand can be all sorts of positions coming from one understanding. It is a willingness to sacrifice everything except your truth, your way of being, your commitment. The ultimate stand is to do something with your life that will make a difference. I learnt from my native ancestry the power of commitment and the magic of bringing something into being. I learnt we are magical in this indefinable world where anything is possible because we are human beings.

Assata Shakur:

I will be honest with you. I hate war in all its forms: physical, psychological, spiritual, emotional.

I hate war and I hate having to struggle. I honestly do because I wish I had been born into world where it was unnecessary. This context of struggle and being a warrior and a struggler has been forced onto me by oppression. Otherwise I would be a sculptor or a gardener, a carpenter; I would be free to be much more. This state of war, this state of oppression is holding us all back. We can't go forward till we get rid of the oppression we are living under, till we rid of that imperialistic octopus that is just taking our life force away.

I guess part of me, of part of who I am, and part of what I do is to be a warrior, a reluctant warrior reluctant struggler. But I do because I am committed to life. We can't avoid it. We can't run away from it because to do that is to be cowardly. To do that is to be subservient to evil. And to do that is to be subservient to the devils, subservient to evil. And so the only way to live on this planet, with any human dignity, at this time, is to struggle. We need to struggle against those who make war against humans, against the earth, we have to struggle against them or otherwise we will be annihilated, the earth will be annihilated. We have no choice.

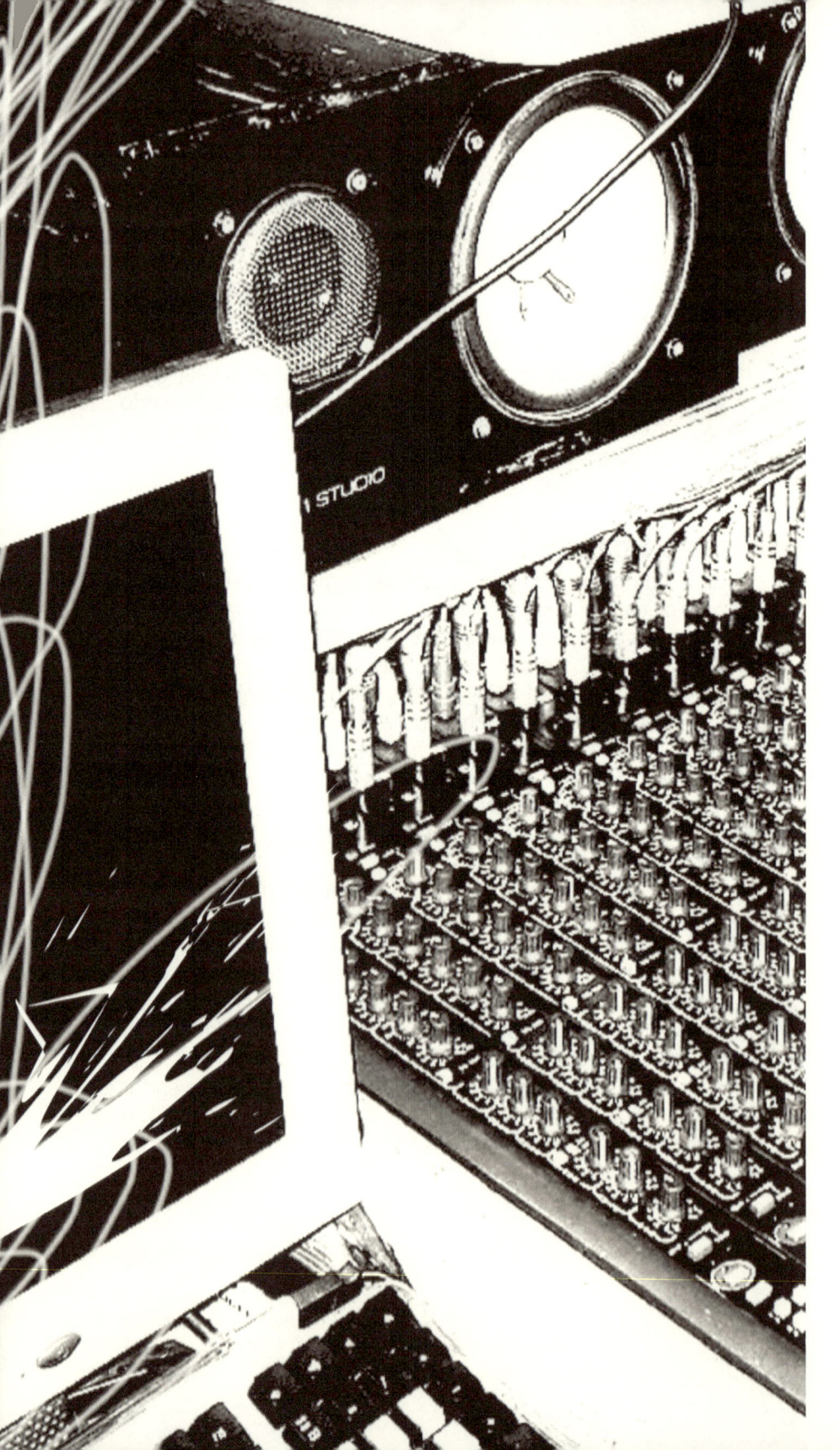

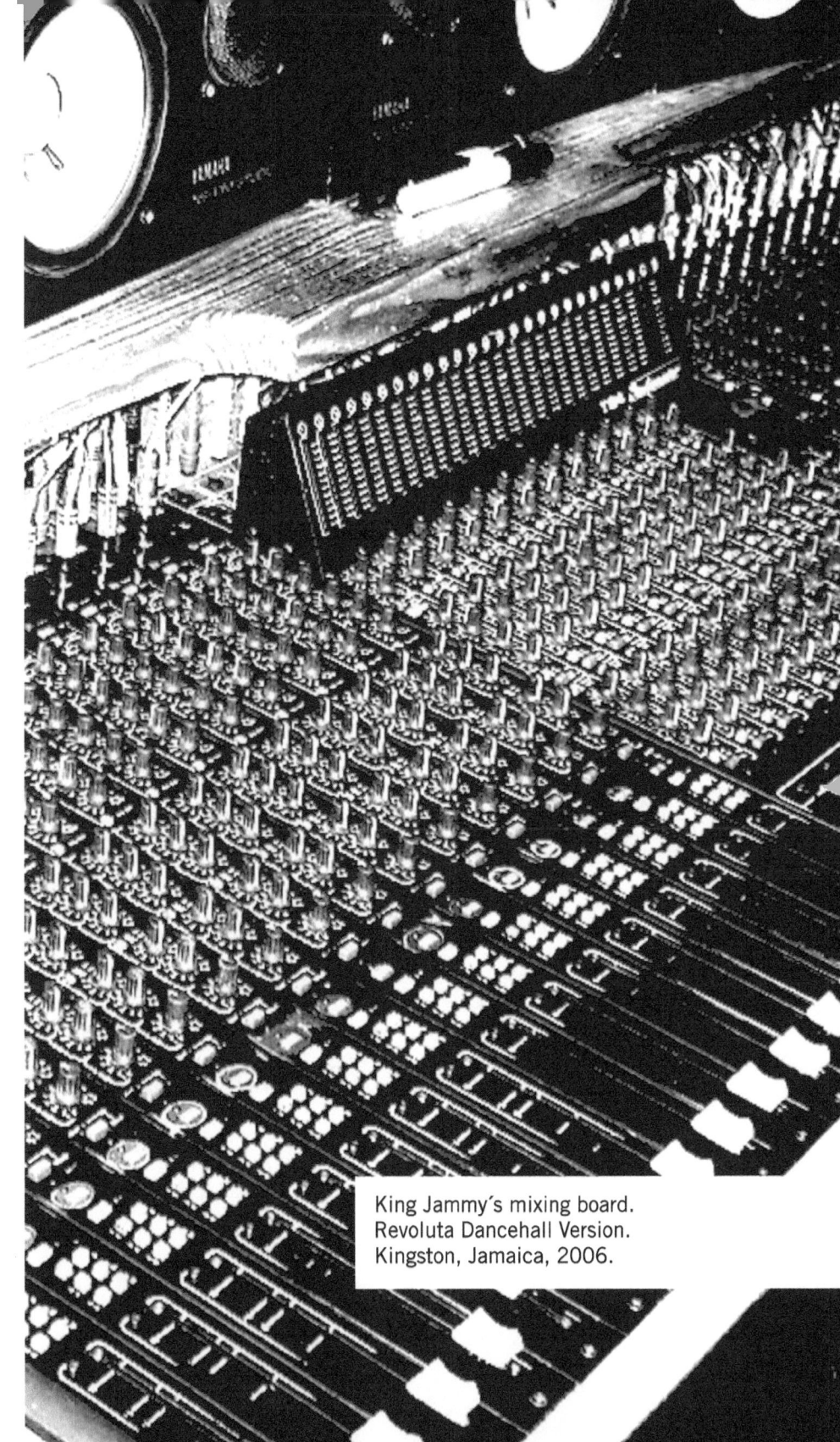

King Jammy's mixing board.
Revoluta Dancehall Version.
Kingston, Jamaica, 2006.

Final Mixes
Discography

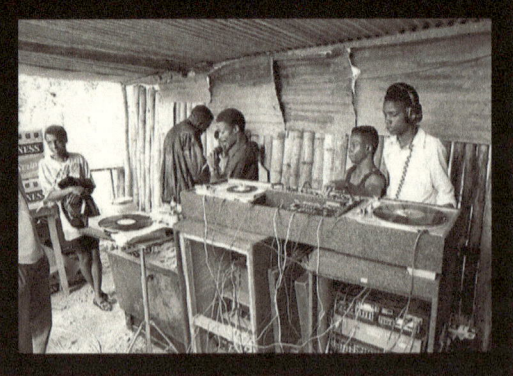

After selecting and editing segments from these nine tracks we then did final mixes. You can listen to these completed tracks and therefore get a further insight into the dub creative process.

John Trudell can be heard on "Poundmakers Dub" from cd "Dancing on John Wayne's Head" by The Fire This Time

---

Assata Shakar can be heard on "Reluctant Warrior" from cd "Still Dancing on John Wayne's Head", "Assata Dub" from cd "IR2" and "Committed To Life" from cd "Community Music" by Asian Dub Foundation.

Pesio and Tohununo can be heard on "Indigenous And... Sacred' from cd "IR2".

Philosophy of Douglas Cardinal and Jeannette Armstrong can be heard on tracks "Basslines and Ballistics" "Beyond Survival Dub" "Waking Dreamer Dub" "No White Borders Dub"/

Some of these tracks are available as free downloads on www.firethistime.com or available from Filter www.dorado.net (extra dub Special Projects vinyl mix of Reluctant Warrior)
& Calabash music http: //thefirethistime.calabashmusic.com

}

Studio Tech Notes

John Trudell recorded during bumpy car ride in New York City.

Assata Shakur recorded in Havana, Cuba.

Pesio and Tuhunnu recorded in Sosolakam and Solomon Islands in the Pacific.

Douglas Cardinal recorded in the hallway of the Museum of Civilization in Hull, Canada.

Philosophical wisdubs from Jeannette Armstrong and Douglas Cardinal on tracks eight and nine can be found in "The Native Creative Process" published by Theytus Books. Those interested in deep basslines should definitely make an effort to access this very rich source.

Binta Breeze can also be accessed from "Understanding the Connections between Black and Aboriginal Peoples" published by the Fire This Time.

Some of poetry by John Trudell in track 3 can be accessed in his cassette "Tribal Voices". Recordings by John Trudell contain an abundance of hidden frequencies well worth tracking down.

Additional Technicians/Studio Personnel

Our dub productions are collaborative projects that rely on technical, dub creativity, critical commentary, support and sheer inspiration from a number of sources. Here are some of them: Dubdem, Bobby Marshall, Tapedave, Jaime Canfield, Eddie, Monique, Dr Das, Sun J, Asian Dub Foundation, Adrian Sherwood, Charlie Lexton, Jaime Lexton, Ollie Buckwell, Crispin Spry Robinson, Michael Franti, Nick Manneseh, Mark Stewart, Mad Mike, UR, Pele Lanier, Mapuchedub, Soy Sos, Christiane D, Bunny Tom Tom, Loretta Collins (title dub), Luana Dub, Apachita Dub, Sinatoka X, Ron Sakolsky, Dandara Dub, Infiltrator Dub, Nikki Dub, Madison Dub, Chan Chan, Prasad Bidaye, Augustus Pablo, Rockers International, Garth Swaby, Muta, Junior Reid, King Jammy Studios, Joe Chang, Jazz, Fijan Sistas Making Trouble, Oku, Night Nurse, Mighty E., Afua, Renegade Radio, Peterman, Henrique & Zumbi Music, Sombra, Rodrigo, Kezia,Lele, Ramjac, Rejane, dj Wattsriot, Frente JDT, MwS, Red Flea, Alice, Lava George, Duran, Toxie, Josiah, Jaabi (he who paints with earth), Jean, Lopes & family, Ni Van story tellers and dub musicians, Kaya Dave, Rich, Timothy, Jenny, Noel & family, Yadira, Fred, Ettienne, Jeremy, Nads, Ck, Allan, Famous Lu, Joana, Fabi, Tecknoassiko, Matar, Touba.

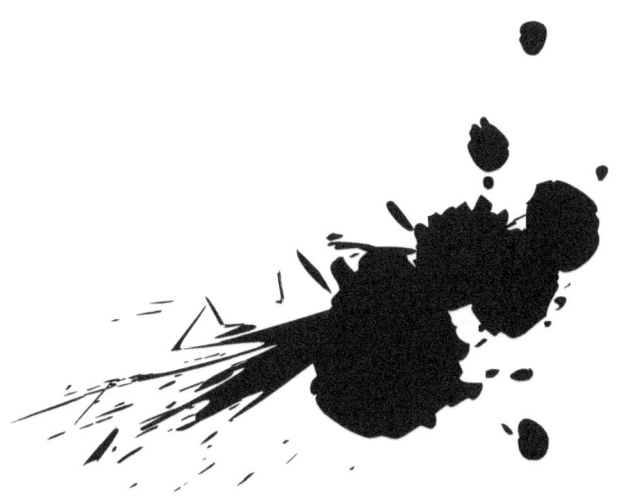

About the Author

Atua Dub is a member of The Fire This Time a collective of black and indigenous artists and activists.

Call on you
Jah nuh Dead
Tumble down
This
Thi
Sla
Mon
Idle   s
Peo
Doo   dy
Cola

Nyah Kidh
Marcus Garvey
Old Marcus
Postman

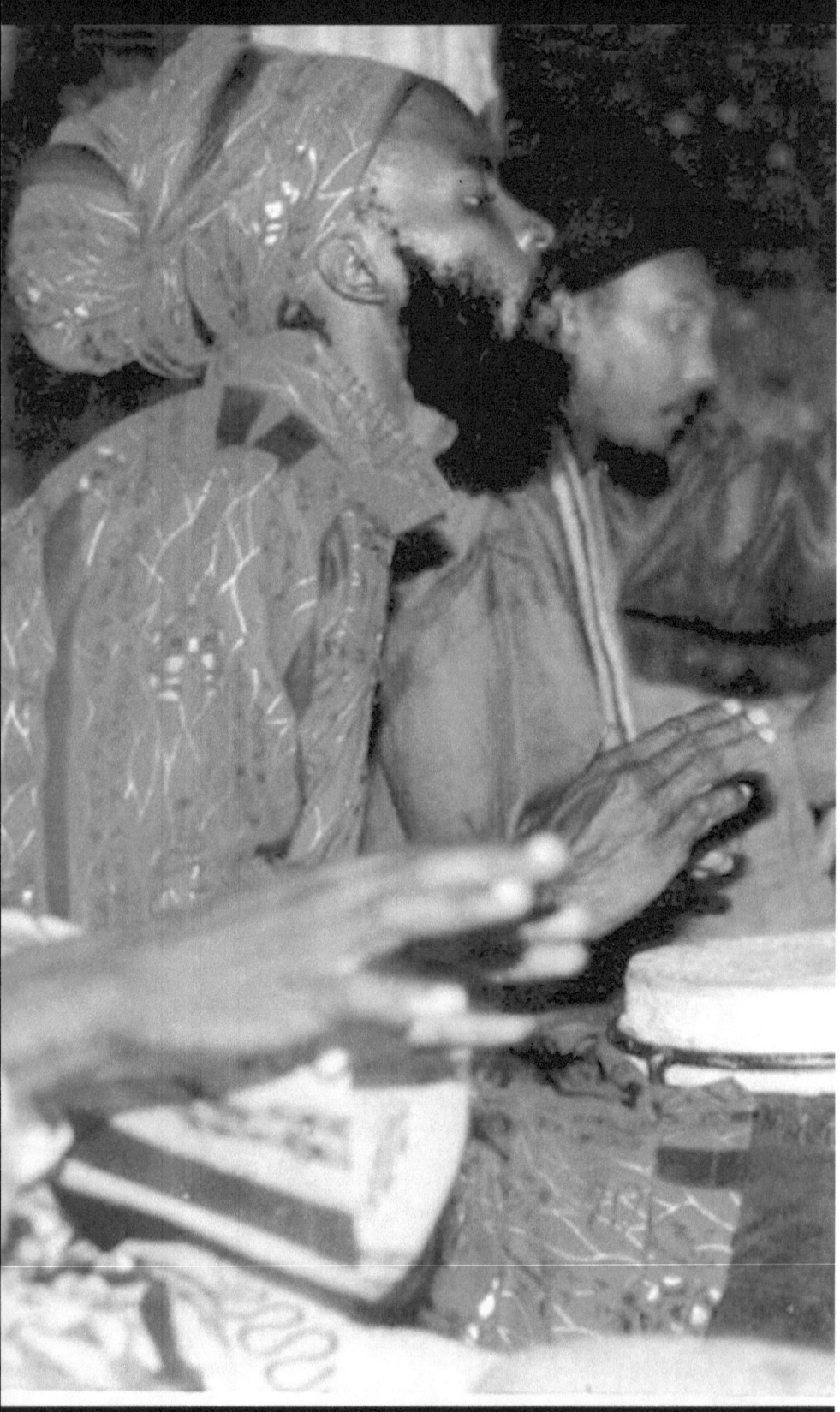

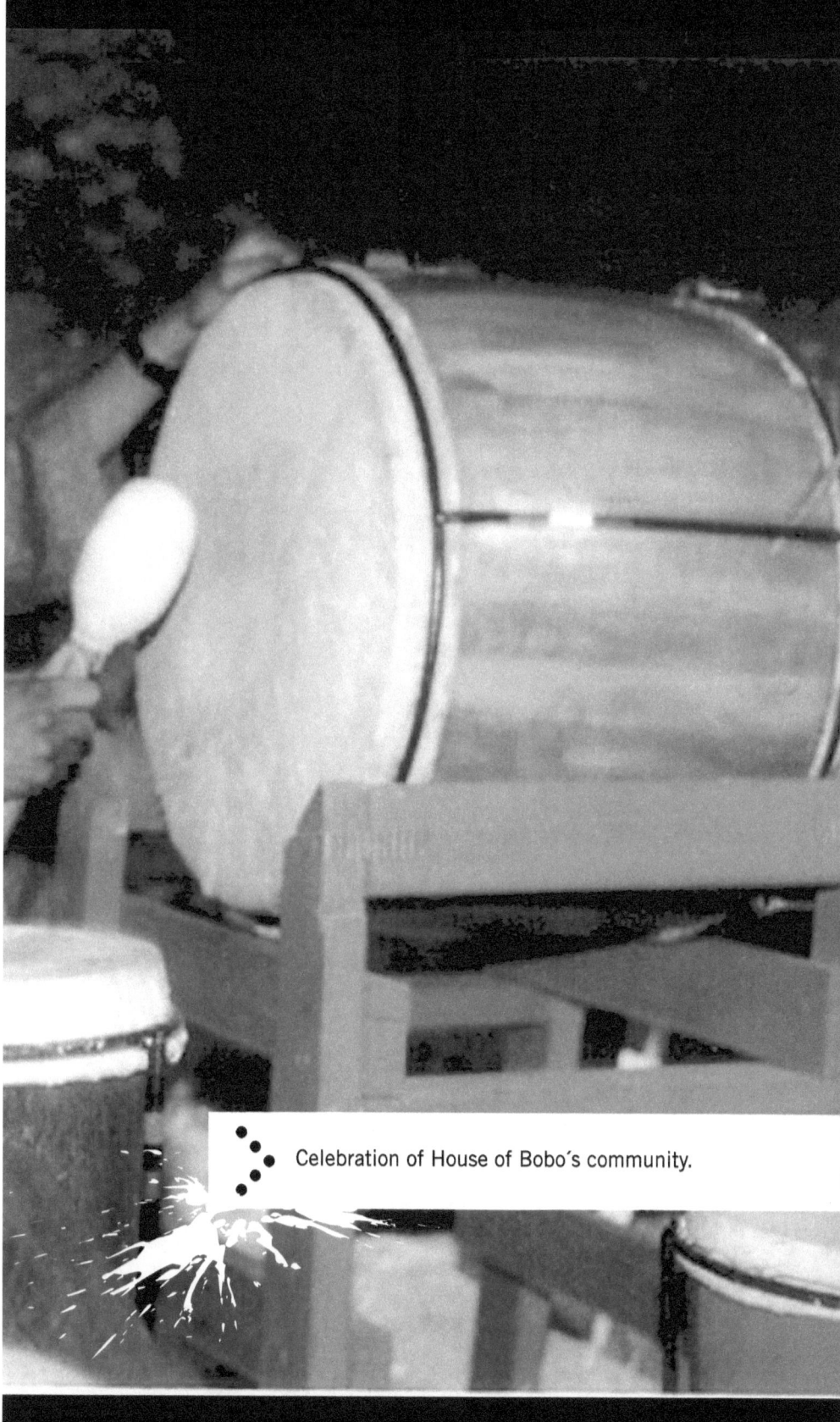
Celebration of House of Bobo's community.

IR9: INDIGENOUSANDBLACKWISDUBS
Indigenous and Black Philosophy & Political Thought.

This book reflects indigenous and black philosophy and political thought that the author gleaned through working with radical indigenous and black people in the Pacific, the Caribbean, Africa and North America. The reader has the opportunity to hear from John Trudell, Assata Shakur, Jeanette Armstrong, Douglas Cardinall, Jean "Binta "Breeze, Tuhunnu and Pesio.

Here are some extracts:
John Trudell
"Leaders know you can't trust one who follows. Followers know not to trust one who leads. They say whoever has the most money has the most power. That's not true, Whoever makes the most money, basically is greedy! They say whoever controls the political vote system that's power. No that's not power. That's exploitation and deceit! But if we believe that these things are power then obviously we don't know ourselves and we don't trust ourselves enough to know that we are connected to the real power source which is life and earth."

Douglas Cardinal
"One has to state that all the premises that men have of women are basically wrong and you start from there. Even the language is wrong. We almost have to recreate a new language which shows respect for women. I think as men if we walked in women's shoes for a while we would be outraged."

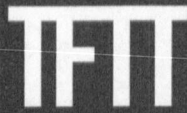

THE VISUAL REVOLUTION

MIX 1

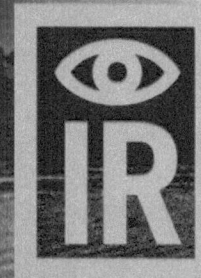

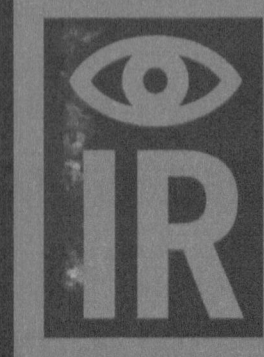

DUTTY BOOKMAN
TRIED & TRUE
REVELATIONS OF A REBELLIOUS YOUTH

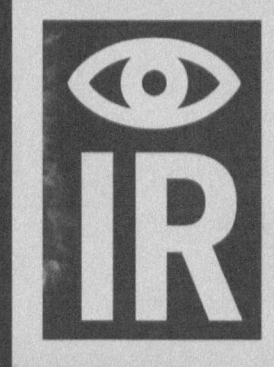

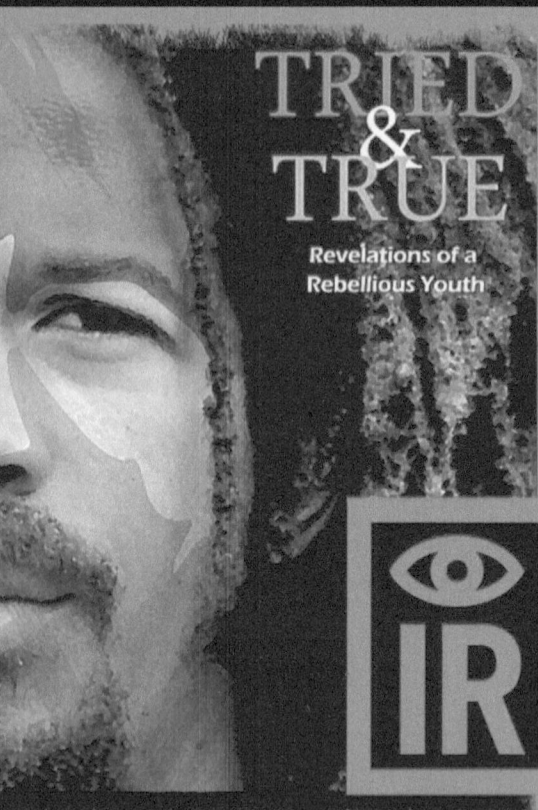

TRIED & TRUE
Revelations of a Rebellious Youth

REVOLUTION
involves being swift, effective and sometimes unexpected.

Wisdom accompanies the individual who fearlessly obeys the impulses within, especially when those impulses pose no foreseeable harm to others.
Dutty Bookman

Leaders know you can't trust one who follows. Followers know not to trust one who leads. They say whoever has the most money has the most power. That's not true. Whoever makes the most money, basically is greedy! They say whoever controls the political vote system that's power. No that`s not power. That's exploitation and deceit! But if we believe these things are power then obviously we don`t know ourselves and we don't trust ourselves enough to know that we are connected to the real power source which is life and earth.
John Trudell

አሰፋት ፈማንነትን ውጤታማነትን እንዲሁም አንዳንዴ ዝ ያልጠበቅነውን ያስከትላል። ፕበብ ውስጣዊ ግፊቱን ኮሚተተል ግለሰብ ጋር ይኑተዳል። በተለይ እነዚህ ግፊቶች ለሌሎች አስቀደም የሚታወቅ ጉዳት በሚያደርስት ሁኔታ ዳቴ ብሉ ግን።

መሪዎች በተከታዮች ላይ እምነት መጣል እንደማይቻል ይውቃሉ ተከታዮች መሪን ማመን እንደሌለባቸው ያውቃሉ ቢሆንም ከሁሉ በላይ ገንዘብ ያለው ከሁሉ በላይ ስልጣን ያለው ነው ይላሉ። ይህ እውነት አይደለም ማንኛውም የገርተኛ ገንዘብ ባለቤት በመሰረቱ ስግብግብ ነው። የፖለቲካውን የድምፅ አሰጣጥ ሥርዓት ባለስልጣን ነው ይላሉ።

ይህ ስልጣን አይደለም ብዝበዛ እና ሸፍጥ ነው። ነገር ግን እነዚህ ነገሮች ስልጣን ናቸው ብለን ካመንን በግልፅ እኛያችንን እናውቅም እንዲሁም በቂ ሁኔታ እራሳችንን እናተማመንም ስለሀኑ ሀይወት እና መሬት ከሆነት እውነተኛ የስልጣን ምንጭ የተሳሰርን መሆናችንን እናውቅም ዳሳስ ካርዴል።

ዐንዶች ሰለፎች ሊናገ ቅድመ ሁሉሞኛው በመሰረቱ የተሳሳተ ናቸው። እንም ከዚህ መጀመር ከለብ ደንቀው እንኳን የተሰሳተ ነው።

ለሰቶች ከበር የሚያመለከት አዲስ ቋንቁ እንደገና የማምላት አለብን ዐንዶች በሴቶች ሳማ ለሞቱት ዝ በሪመዳ እጅግ በጣም እንቦሳዋ ነበር።

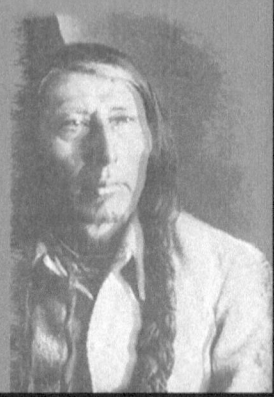

One has to state that the premises that men have of women are basically wrong and start from there. Even the language is wrong. We almost have to recreate a new language that shows respect for women. I think as men if we walked in women's shoes for a while we would be outraged.
Douglas Cardinal

MARCUS GARVEY

said to read. Knowledge is the key. I know this is true from my own experience. I am not afraid to admit to anyone that I am coming from a state of complete ignorance. My ignorance still exists in many ways today, but each time I pick up a book, complete it and put it down, I feel more powered with my next breath. Knowledge is power.
Dutty Bookman

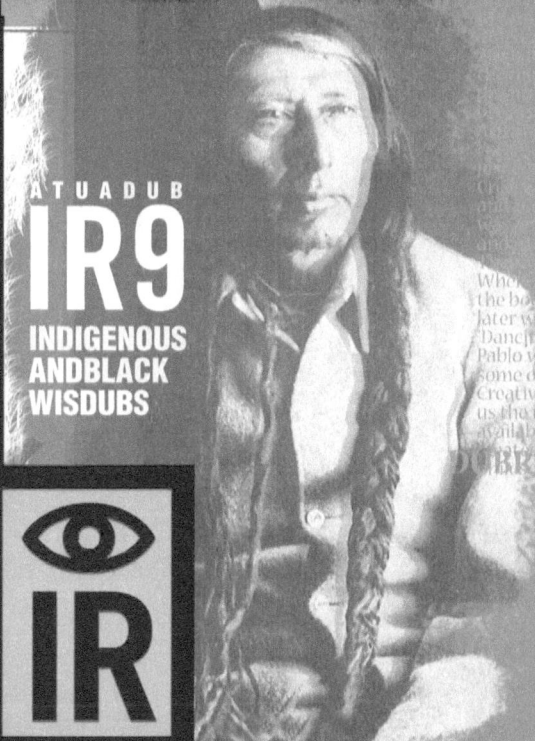

ATUADUB
IR9
INDIGENOUS ANDBLACK WISDUBS

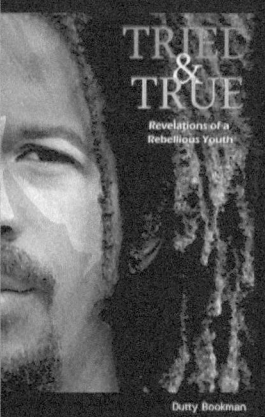

አበሎት ረባናትን ሙጪታማነትን እንዲሁም አገዛዝ ዝቢ ያልጠየቀውን ያስከትላል። የበዘ ሙሰባዊ ንፅፈት ከሚተላ ግለሰብ ጋር ይነጉሳል። በተለይ እነዚህ ግፊቶች ለሴሎች እስትጀም የሚፈፀሙ ጉዳት በሚያደርሱበት ሁኔታ ዳቱ ብቦ ማን።

መረጃዎች በተለያዮች ላይ እምነት መማል እንደማይቻል ያውቃሉ ተዛምያዎች ወሬን ማመን እንደለሰባቸው ያውቃሉ ቢሆንም ከሁሉ በላይ የገዛ ያለቡ ከዛባ በላይ ስልጣን ያለው ነው ይባል። ይህ እውነት አደደለም ማንኛውም የክፋተኝ ግዘዛ ባለቤት በመሰረቱ ስግብግብ ነው የፖለቲክውን የዶምይ እሳዋዋ ስርነት ባለሰልጣን ነው ይላል።

ይህ ስልጣን አይደለም ብዘሀ እና ሸዋዋ ነው። ነገር ግን እነዚህ ነገሮች ስልጣን ናፎው ብለን ከወደን በግሌል እስስፉንን እናውቅም እንዲሁም በቱ ሁኔታ እራሳችንን አገዛማወንም ስለዚህ ሀይወት እና ሙፈት ከዞነት እውነተኛ የስልጣን ምንጭ የተሰበረን መሀናችን እናውቅም ሳንስ ካርደናል።

ወገድት ስለሶቶች ስናና ቀድሙ ሁሰያቸው በመሰረቱ የተሳሳቴ ናቸው። እናም ከዚሁ ሙጀሙር ካለቡ ድንቁሮ እንኗ.ነ የተሳሳተ ነው።

ስሱሎት ከቦር የሚያሙስስት አዲስ ቋንቋ አንዳና የማምዋት አልብን ወንድጀ በሱሎት ላሚ ለየቴት ንቢ ቢታሙል አሰን በዓም እንበሳዋ ዘር።

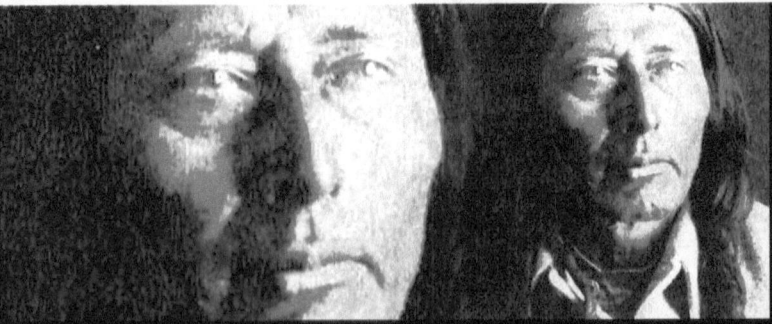

GALDINO JESUS DOS SANTOS
PATAXÓ WARRIOR
A LUTA POR JUSTIÇA CONTINUA

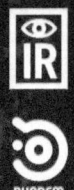

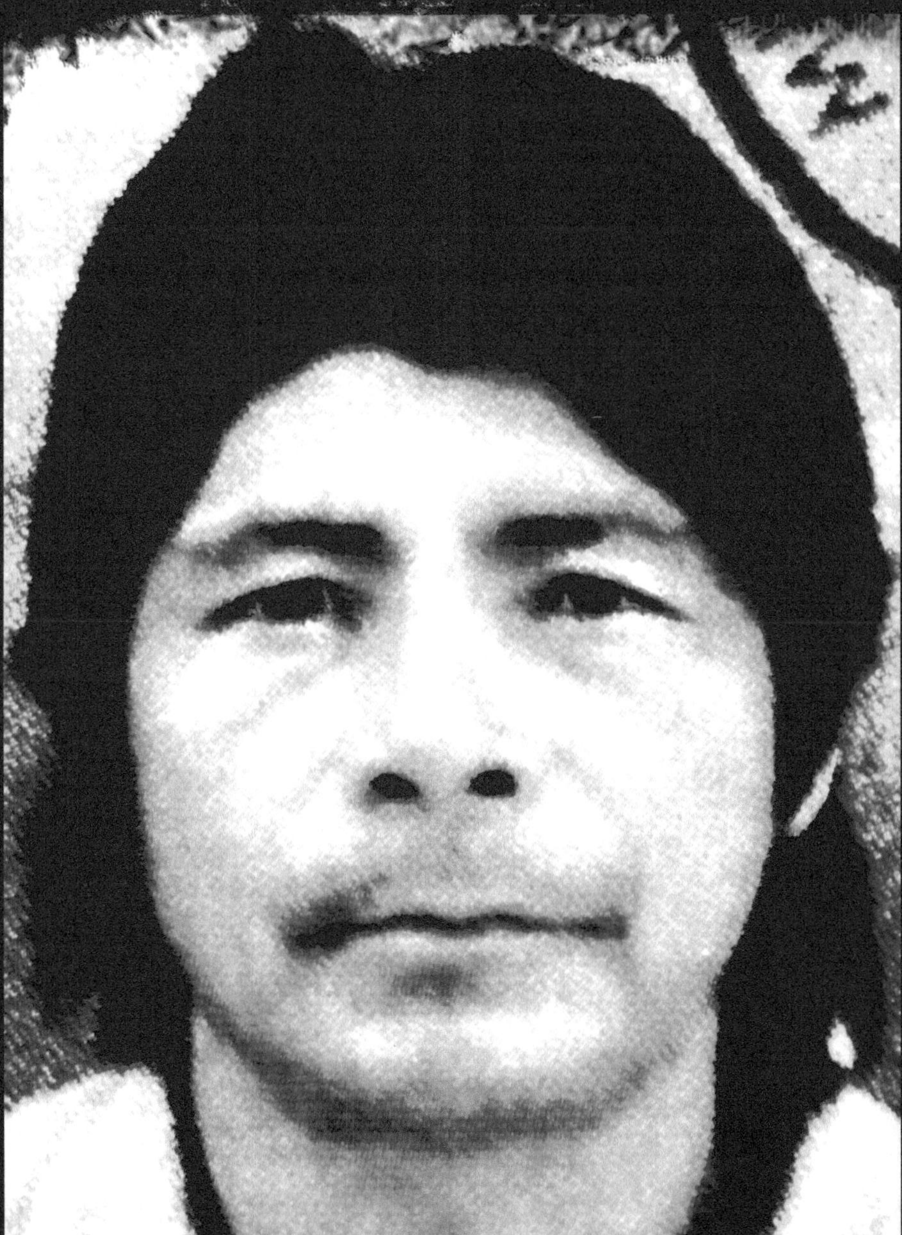

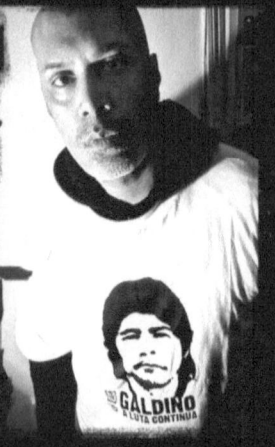 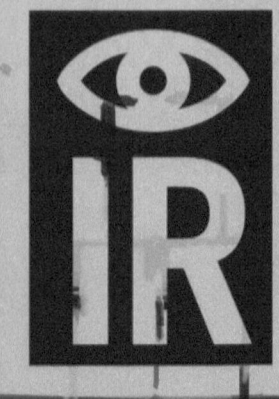 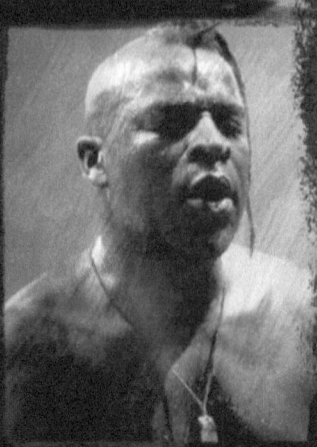

IR27   THE JAMAICAN :: HAWAII MIXES
SHADOW WARS
WWW.DUBREALITY.COM

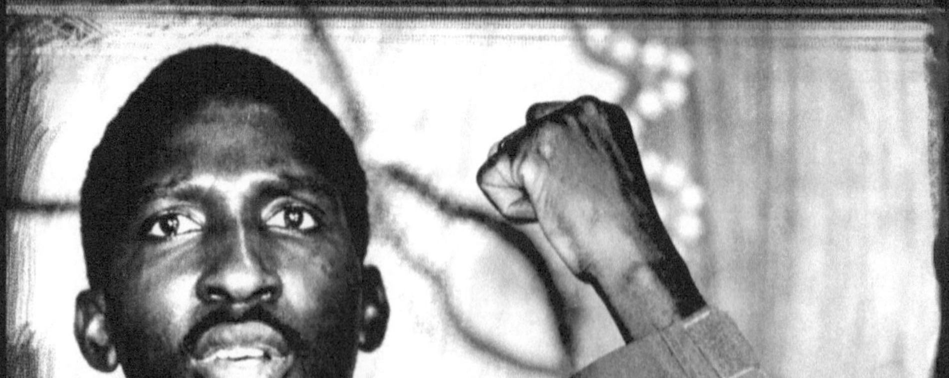

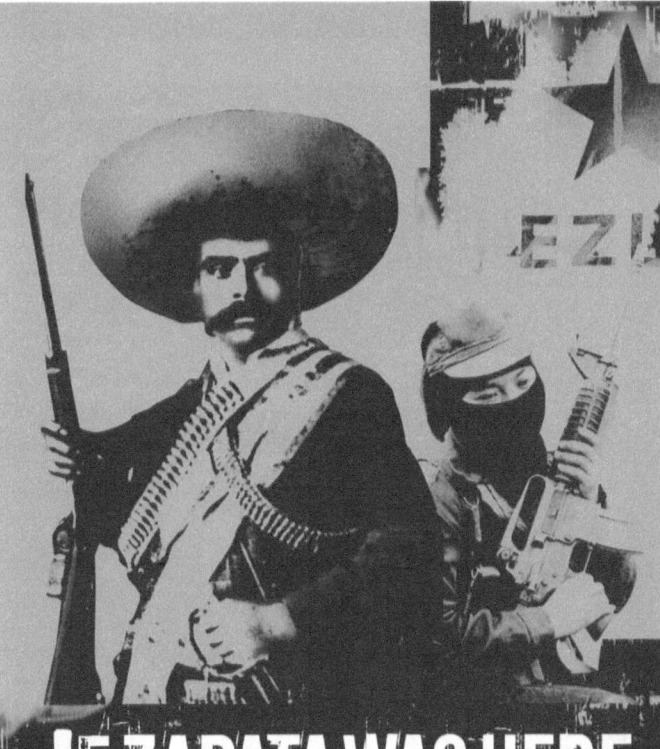

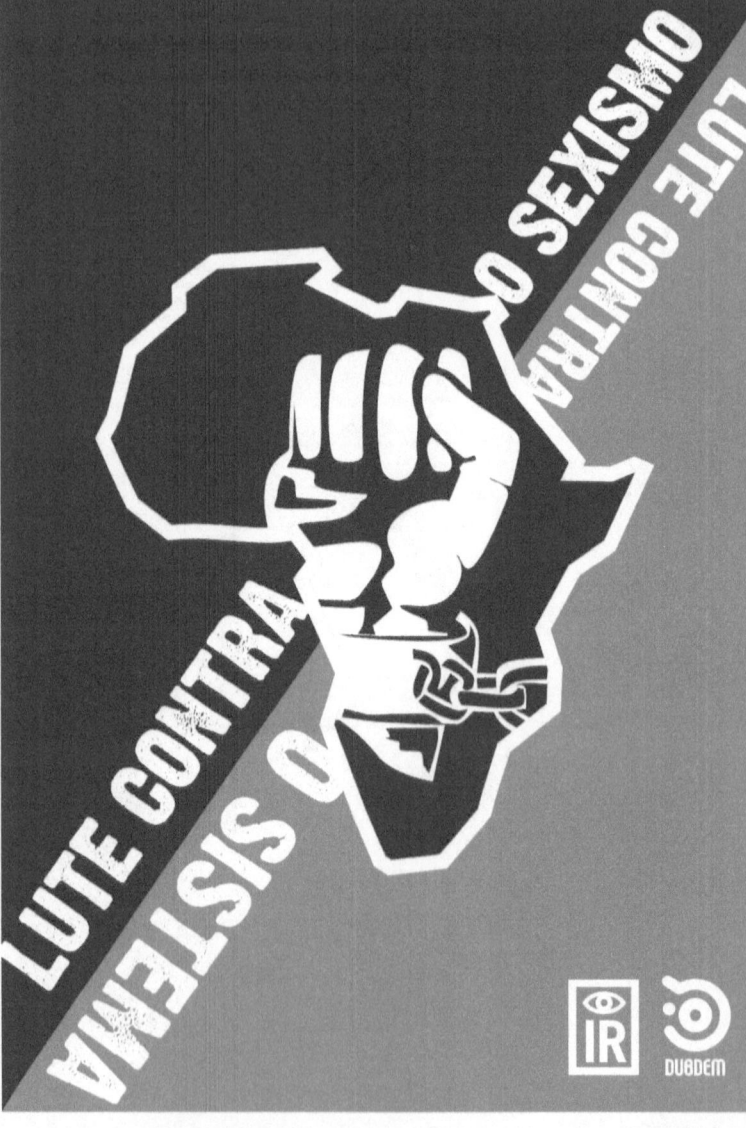

FREE MUMIA ABU JAMAL

I CONTINUE TO FIGHT AGAINST THIS UNJUST SENTENCE AND CONVICTION

I CAN
I WILL

FROM DEATH ROW

EVEN IF I MUST DO SO FROM THE VALLEY OF SHADOW OF DEATH

MUMIA ABU JAMAL

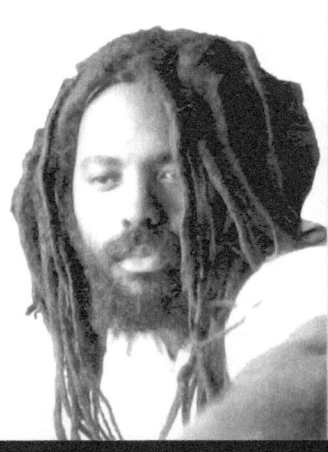

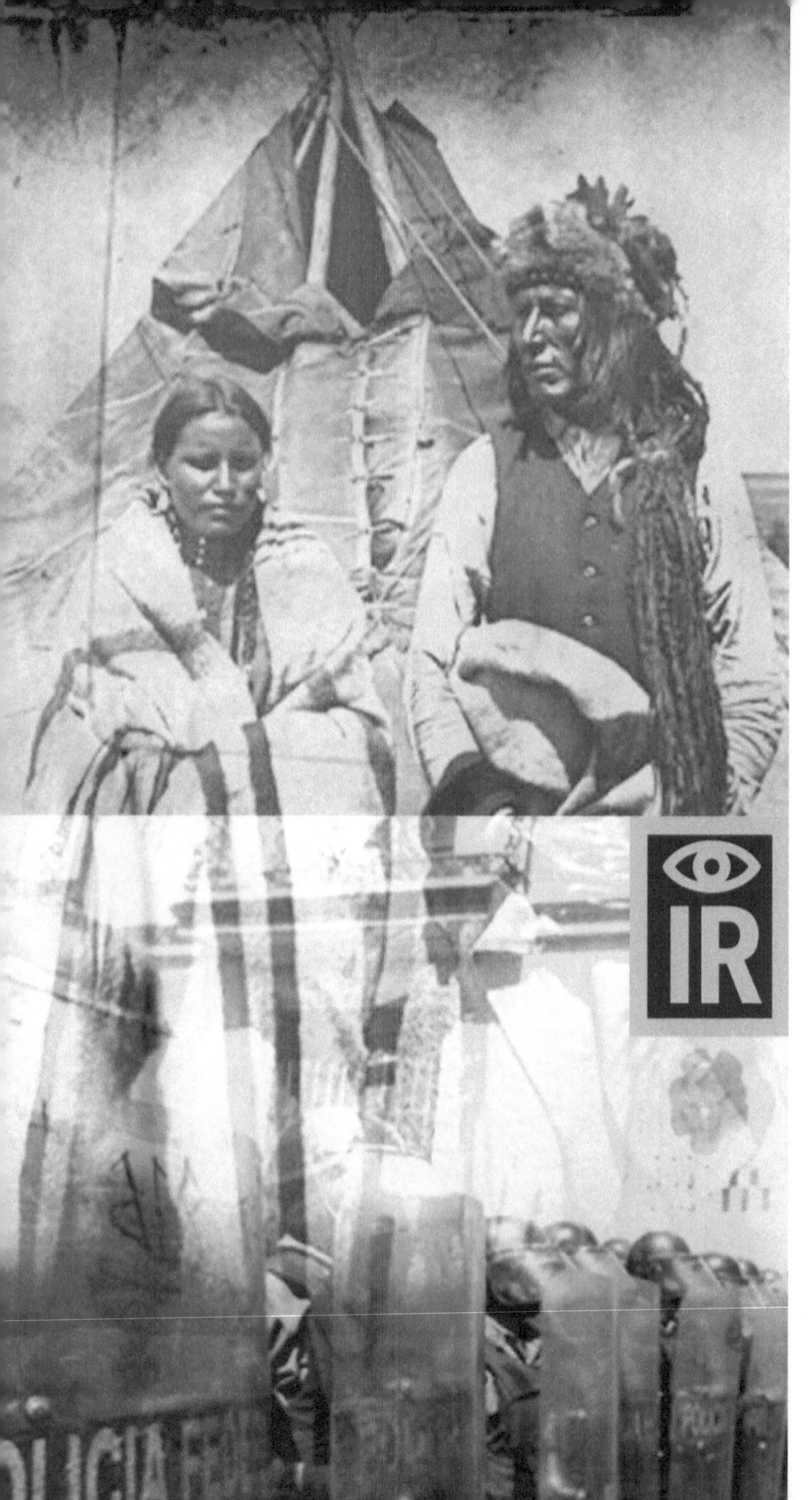

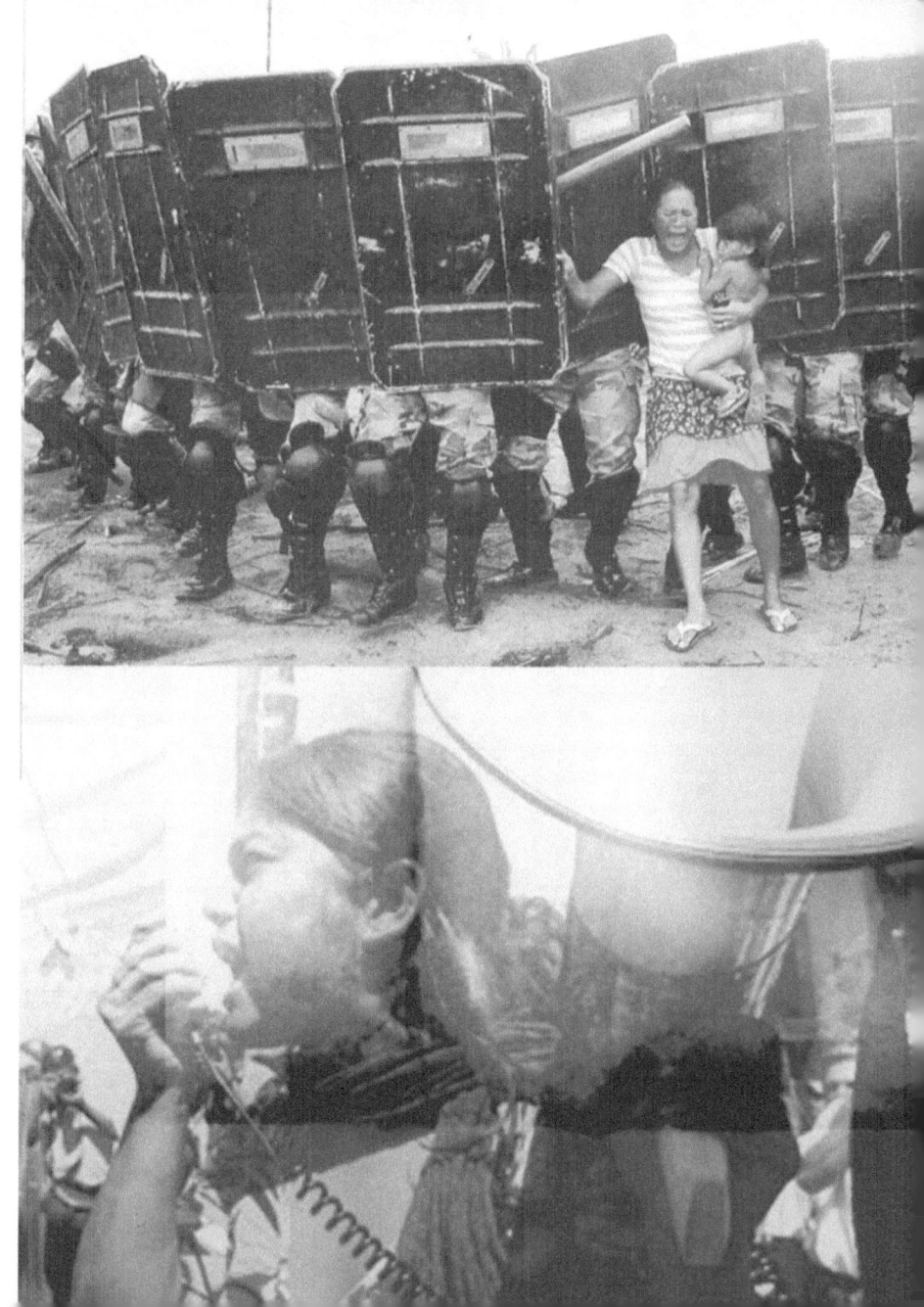

"The true owners of your nation are forced to live on a reservation." —Mutabaruka

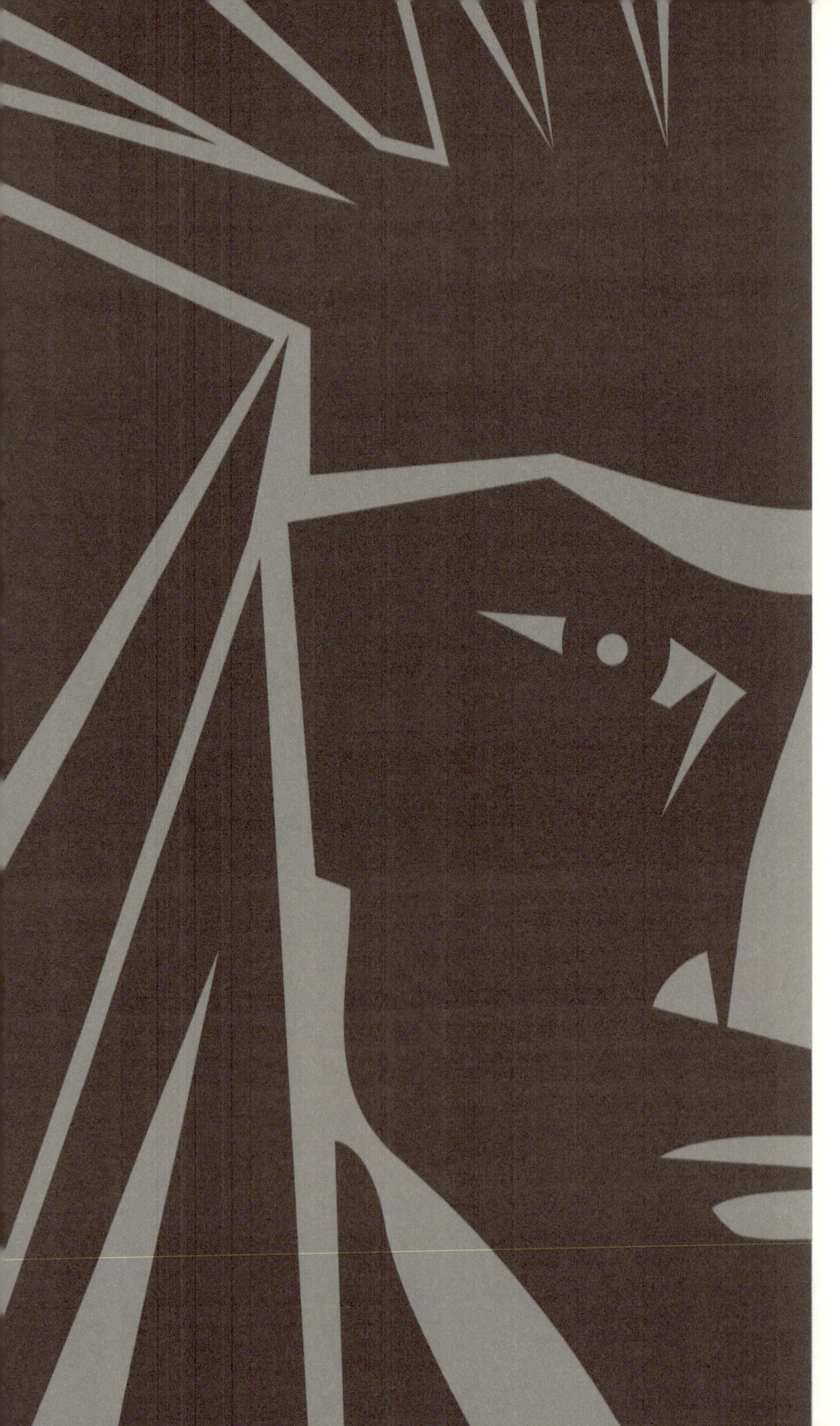

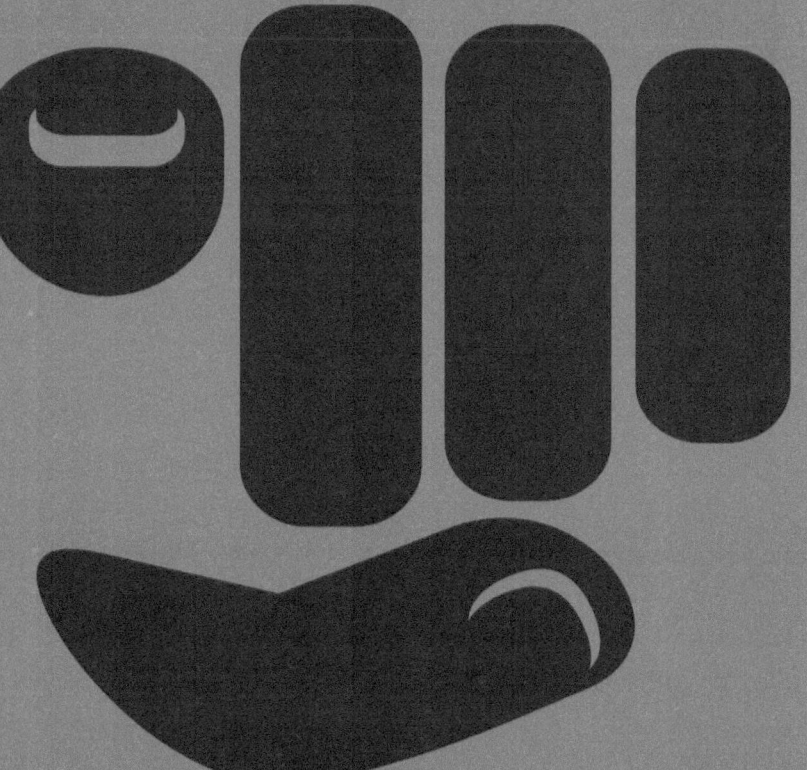

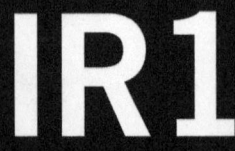

> **The following is the text of the liner notes included in a free blue vinyl release IR1 written in January 2003.** We have included it because as our Brasilian comrades Labomb say "Brasil is a country without memory" and we feel it's important to reflect on the attitudes that existed 10 years ago before the emergence of issues like the Bel Monte Dam.

Maybe it was the angry expression on my face that made this indigenous woman speak to me. There I was at the Museu De Republica in Rio De Janeiro at a performance involving various indigenous peoples in honour of the fact that it was DAY OF THE INDIOS.

From my point of view it seemed like a parade of all the acceptable stereotypes and images of indigenous people. Feathers, paint, indigenous people dancing in a circle, playing indigenous instruments. In a day that was supposed to inform the public about the situation of indigenous people what was striking was what the public wasn't being told. Information boards around the museum talked about customs, cooking utensils, fishing hooks.... but there was no mention of disputes by indigenous people to reclaim their land, to have their ancestral territorial boundaries respected. No mention of how when the Portuguese arrived in Brasil there were over two thousand indigenous languages now there's only slightly over two hundred. No mention of how so many indigenous peoples were murdered. How so many cultures were decimated.

On a very personal note for me there was absolutely no mention of Galdino Jesus Dos Santos. This Patoxi warrior had gasoline poured on him when was he asleep on a sidewalk by the sons of prominent lawyers and judges in Brasilia. Galdino was thenset on fire by Max Rogério Alves, Antônio Novely Cardoso Vilanova, Tomás Oliveira de Almeida and Eron Chaves Oliveira. He died from third degree burns to ninety percent of his body. I never saw Galdino's face but when I went to the trial of the four accused of murdering him, his family showed me the coroners photos of his horribly burnt corpse. It was something I would never forget.

Yet at this event supposedly honoring indigenous people there was absolutely nothing remembering the life lost of this innocent man. Instead what was being being forced into public consciousness was the image of the quaint exotic indigenous person. Invisible, non-existent except in obscene caricatures on soap operas and at carnival. Beads, feathers, handicrafts these were the symbols allotted to indigenous people. A middle class Brazilian woman walked in front of me. She was loaded down with an assortment of indigenous beads and necklaces she had bought from vendors.

I said what do you think of the fact there's nothing here to remember Galdino. She stopped, gave me her full attention and with a beautiful smile, innocently asked

"GALDINO? WHO'S THAT?"

Angry I turned my back to her and walked away. I started thinking about the indifference I perceived to indigenous issues, even with all the media that Galdino's case received no one I asked could tell me the name of an entire music that solely dealt with what happened to Galdino.

Editor's note * In response to this indifference I.R. subsequently organised and produced tracks that focused on what happened to Galdino including a free vinyl IRI

Someone pointed out a pseudo hip hop video that had a reference to Galdino. But this video was full of stereotyped racist references to indigenous people. The video contained various scenes of painted indigenous people sitting around a fire. To me this was one of the most clichéd images of indigenous people, perpetuating the image of indigenous people as animal like people limited to a life of just sitting around the fire in the jungle. But indigenous people are more than that; I thought of an indigenous friend of mine who was a computer programmer and hacker, another who was a lawyer and got totally pissed off. Pushing this stereotype of indigenous people totally destroyed any good intention the artist might have had. I kept asking myself where

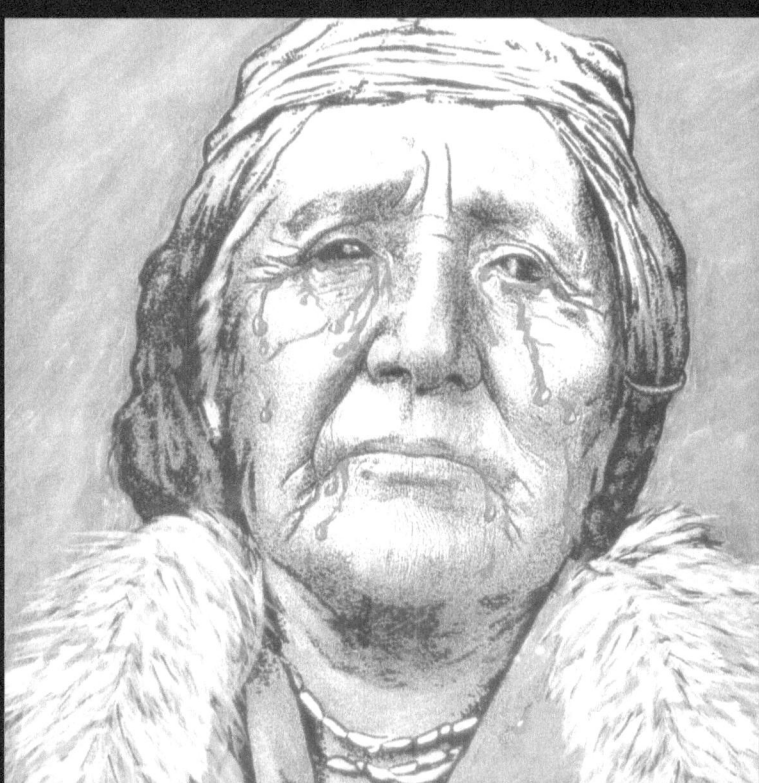

were the voices of the artists and musicians speaking out about **this tragedy that occurred with Galdino.**

Where were the voices speaking out about the way the serious life threatening issues of indigenous peoples. Their issues were practically never discussed. Its as if indigenous people don't exist. Their issues don't count. When I travelled around Brasil and talk with Brazilians and artists about this, people were usually sympathetic but there was always an attitude of indifference. Often I walked away feeling like I was talking to people about something they really didn't feel was that important. Not that it didn't matter but there were things way more important to discuss and work on. Talking about indigenous people well that was something left to gringos like Sting who like to go to the Amazon and take photos besides painted indians.

It was at this moment with my heart both angry and sad at the lack of remembrance for Galdino that this indigenous woman approached me. She was as angry about the event as I was. People are very happy to come to an event like this she said. They see painted exotic indigenous people playing music and dancing. They think ah we have seen the real indians the ones that live in the jungle. But almost every big city has indigenous people living in it. There's a favela (ghetto) of São Paulo that's full of Guarani Indians. Are you telling me those aren't real indians? I asked her what she thought was the reason for the indifference shown to indigenous people and their issues.

She replied somehow we are programmed to see Brazilian indians as inferior to "civilized people" and to "imported indians" like the American indians. They have this mystic this glamour. They are more beautiful than Brazilian indians. People love tattoos with American indians.

Brazilan indians are seen like old old buildings that shouldn't be destroyed because they represent a piece of the nations history. They are seen almost like extinct animals. People don't care if they are living or how they are Living. Theres more noise made about about an old building about to be torn down than

ESTES SÃO OS CRETINOS QUE MATARAM GALDINO

MAX ROGÉRIO ALVES
ANTÔNIO NOVELY CARDOSO VILANOVA
TOMÁS OLIVEIRA DE ALMEIDA
ERON CHAVES OLIVEIRA

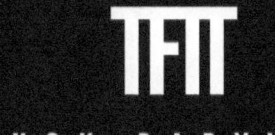

FUCK BABYLON

THESE FOUR BASTARDS MURDERED GALDINO

MAX ROGÉRIO ALVES
ANTÔNIO NOVELY CARDOSO VILANOVA
TOMÁS OLIVEIRA DE ALMEIDA
ERON CHAVES OLIVEIRA

TFTT

FUCK BABYLON

say when a group of indigenous people are murdered by cattle ranchers who want their land to raise cattle.

She reached into her bag and pulled out a photo. She said I'm going to show you something that runs counter to all the stereotype of indigenous people, she showed me a photo of a group of indigenous women some were masked, all were carrying rifles. I'm not trying to glamorize guns here, the media is always doing this. I know in this situation these indigenous women have guns because they are in a desperate situation and they were forced to defend themselves.

But the reason I am showing you this is because it goes completely against the image of indigenous people as passive people always willing to accept the misery and oppression they often face. The public doesn't think of Brazilian indians as people ready and willing to fight back. Most Brazilians would get really surprised if I show them this photo. On this point I really agreed with her. I told aboutthe Krikati indians of Maranho who fought back against the government and hydroelectric companies ,destroying powerlines that had been erected on their land and knocking out power in major cities. Their actions forced the government who ignored years of their attempts at peaceful negotiations to finally pay attention to their need for territorial demarcation.

A courageous action by a small nation of people but something that is not discussed. The image of passive indigenous people is so powerful yet the Zapatistas of Mexico are applauded by many in Brasil and many wear Zapatista t-shirts but I often ask myself if these folks are aware of the fact that many Zapatistas are in fact indigenous people. Additionally there are indigenous people involved in resistance movements in various parts of the world.

Editors note *some years after this article was written the general Brazilian public's perception of indigenous people got a rude shock as indigenous anger over assassinations, total disregard for their ancestral and territorial rights boiled over and indigenous people put up roadblocks, barricades as part of protests. These protests were difficult to ignore even though it was interesting to see how often the connation of "savagery" was applied to the protests.

When I mentioned this she pulled out a magazine. She said look at this magazine, it has some good information on indigenous people in Brasil, however look very carefully who publishes it. This magazine is done by missionaries. We can't forget missionaries have an agenda. They are on a mission to convert. We can't deny the assistance they give to indigenous communities doing work that no one is else is doing. But we have to ask ourselves why is no one else doing this work?. Where are the people from the left and progressive movements. How is the 'left' have allowed the church to gain so much access and power with indigenous communities here in Brasil(yet these same 'leftists' will often complain how christianised indigenous people have become). We can't forget the role the missionaries played in the history of the slaughter of indigenous people. They aided the Spanish and Portuguese conquistadors as they tried to eliminate indigenous cultures. To stop indigenous people from being 'heathens'; they imposed their language and religion on them. We know many indigenous women and children were and still are sexually abused by missionaries and priests. I have an Indigenous friend who is now in the process of suing the church. She along with other members of her family had been sexually abused by catholic priests.

She stopped and laughed. You know maybe that's why the church talks so much about the importance of forgiveness. They know all the shit they have done!

After we laughed at this she continued. The point is indigenous people need to own and control their magazines and we need to talk more about the difficult realities we face. We need to address the extreme poverty, suicides, gringos coming in to steal our herbal and medicinal knowledge, lack of land, the land that was stolen from us. We never signed legal documents giving the Portuguese the right to our land and resources.One day when we have more indigenous lawyers we will challenge this in court.Then they will be afraid.

We need to talk about indigenous reality. indigenous resistance. Because some of us are fighting back!

As we write these words a friend sends us an email saying that in the period of ten days 3 indigenous people have been murdered in Brasil:

6 January 2003:: in Rio Grande De Sul.
3 guys kicked to death Leopoldo Crespo a Caiagangue indian who was sleeping on a sidewalk.

9 january :: Aldo de Silva A Macuxi indian was killed in Roraima

14 january :: Marcos Vernon a cacique Guarani-Caiui was killed in regards to a land conflict between indigenous people and ranchers in Mato Grosso Du Sul

She also informed me that the guys who murdered Galdino were now back on the streets after receiving minimal punishment. We need to understand what happened to Galdino is not an isolated incident. From our perspective these incidents reflect a sentiment that the lives of indigenous people are regarded as not as valuable as those of other citizens.

We need to remember those murdered have families who will weep for them. They too like all other Brasilians had the potential to make a contribution

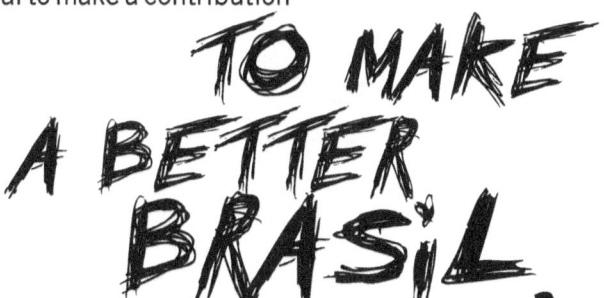

TO MAKE A BETTER BRASIL.

THIS DUB IS FOR GALDINO

BY KOKONDA DUB

An IR/Labomb Art Action where a giant banner of Galdino was clandestinely placed on top of this building in Lapa, Rio de Janeiro, Brasil.

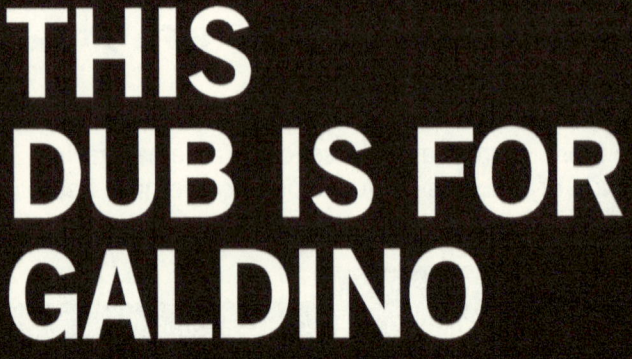

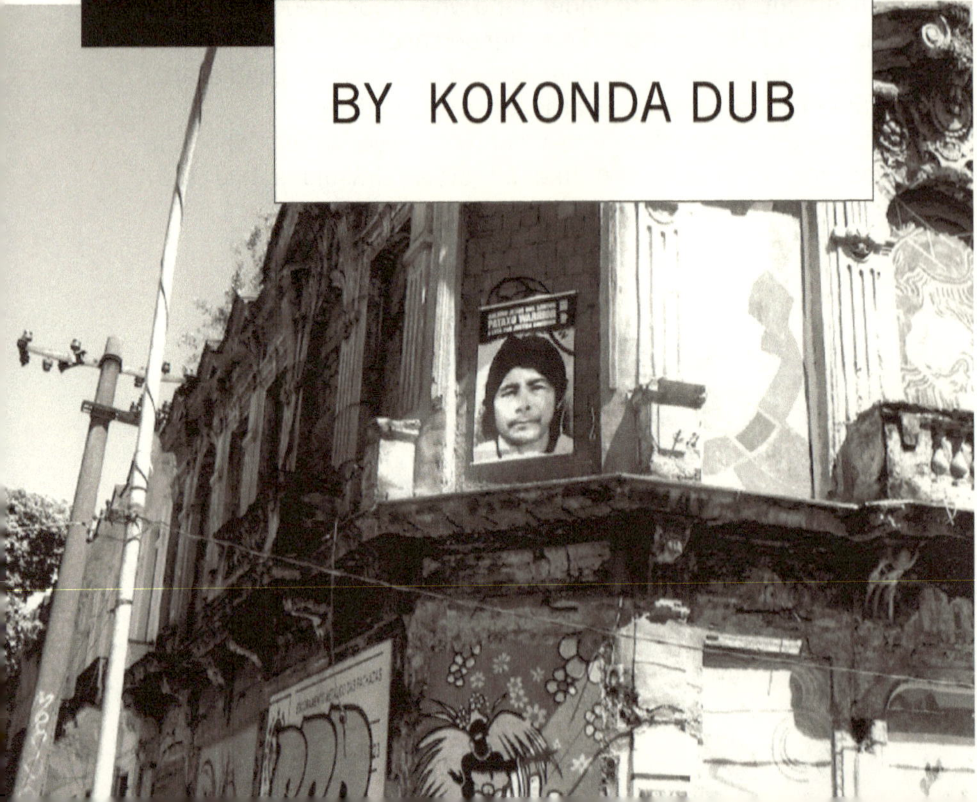

I am standing on the steps of the courthouse in Brasilia. Almost mockingly is a large banner on a fence that says "Land and Justice for Indigenous People" Indigenous people from around Brasil have gathered here for the trial of four of the wealthy youth accused of the murder of a Patoxi Indian, Galdino in 1997. Galdino was in Brasilia at that time for an indigenous meeting. Unable to find lodging he was asleep on a sidewalk when the youth poured gasoline on the sleeping Galdino and lit him on fire.

HE DIED FROM BURNS TO 90% OF IS BODY.

As it happened just as I arrived the coroners photos of Galdino's burnt body are being shown to his family. All around me indigenous people are crying as they see the photos for the first time. One of the many indigenous youth present at the trial approaches me. Even though his face is painted red and he is wearing a headdress of vibrant blue feathers it's the sense of quiet but very strong determination that he exudes that really catches my attention. He says I know you want to understand what's happening here you can take a look at these. He hands me the photos of Galdino horribly burnt corpses. Words can't describe how horrifying a sight it is.

Yet the defence of the youth is that it was just a joke. Among some of their utterances they thought it was just a homeless person. They were setting on fire. The children of judges and wealthy families of Brasil's capital the four youth have been in special cells till the time of the trial. In contrast to the tiny cramped dirty cells with cold showers and no amenities that other inmates are forced to live in the four youth share on extra large cell. With a colour TV, weights, hot showers, desks, special lights and a window without bars to let sunlight in.

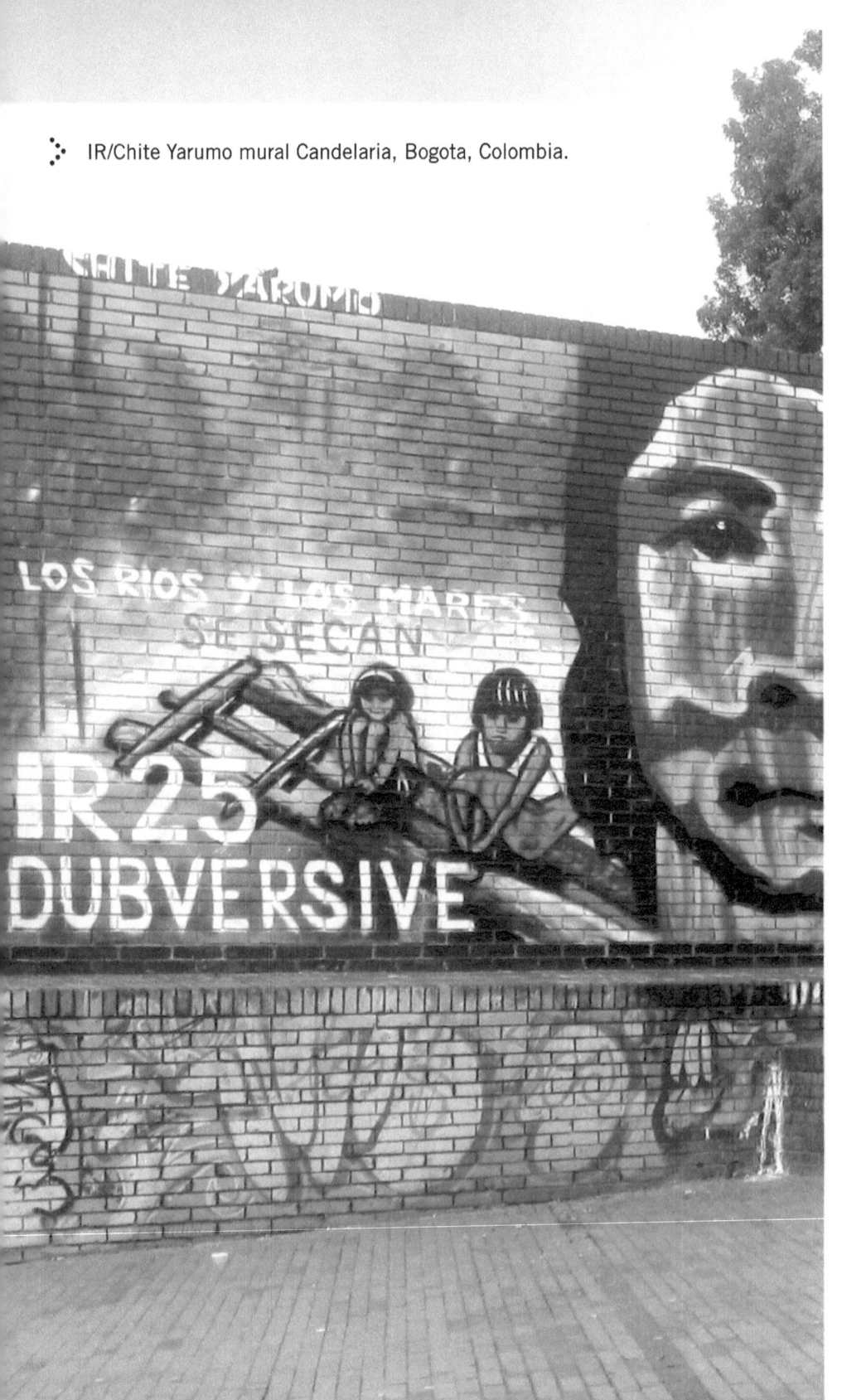

IR/Chite Yarumo mural Candelaria, Bogota, Colombia.

GALDINO

LA TIERRA NO ESTA EN VENTA

LA COMIDA
EL AGUA

During the trial the mother of one of the accused leaves the courthouse weeping. A journalist comments on this to Galdinos mother Minervina. I am perturbed by the tone of the question suddenly it as if the accused are suddenly the victims.

However Mirnervina replies in a defiant manner

"I WANT HER TO CRY, COMPARED TO WHAT I HAVE SUFFERED SHE HASN'T SUFFERED ANYTHING".

She can still see her children. I will never see my son again. The stereotype of indigenous people being oh so ready to forgive and forget receives a body blow at this moment. The sentence is handed down. The accused are given a minimal sentence and in fact soon aftter are back on the streets.

A few days later I'm in the city of Sao Luis in another state. It has really struck me that when I talk to Brasilians about the trial everyone is horrified and very sympathetic to the family of Galdino. I also notice not one person I talk with mentions the deeper issue of the right of indigenous people to land.

Yet of all interactions the one that stuck most in my mind was the response of a middle-aged travel agent. When I mentioned that I was in Brasilia for the trial the man stopped what he was doing and took off his glasses. Suddenly I notice a very far away look in his eyes. He said I don't believe prison solves anything in fact I believe people leave worse than when they came in, but I can't agree with that sentence. Can you imagine if it had been the other way around and a Patoxi burnt one of these rich kids to death; they would get the maximum twenty years; that's if they even managed to stay alive till the time of the trial. You know I was told that there is a man who was serving a five-year jail sentence alongside hardened criminals because one day he was poor and starving and he killed a turtle for something to eat. I believe in protecting the turtles but five years in prison... We both stop and pause. He looks at me with the far away look still in his eyes and says this makes me think about questions of justice.

YOU CAN LISTEN TO THIS TEXT SET ON MUSIC "GALDINO", CREATED BY OF ASIAN DUB FOUNDATION AND FOUND ON THE ALBUM "IR 15 REVOLTA

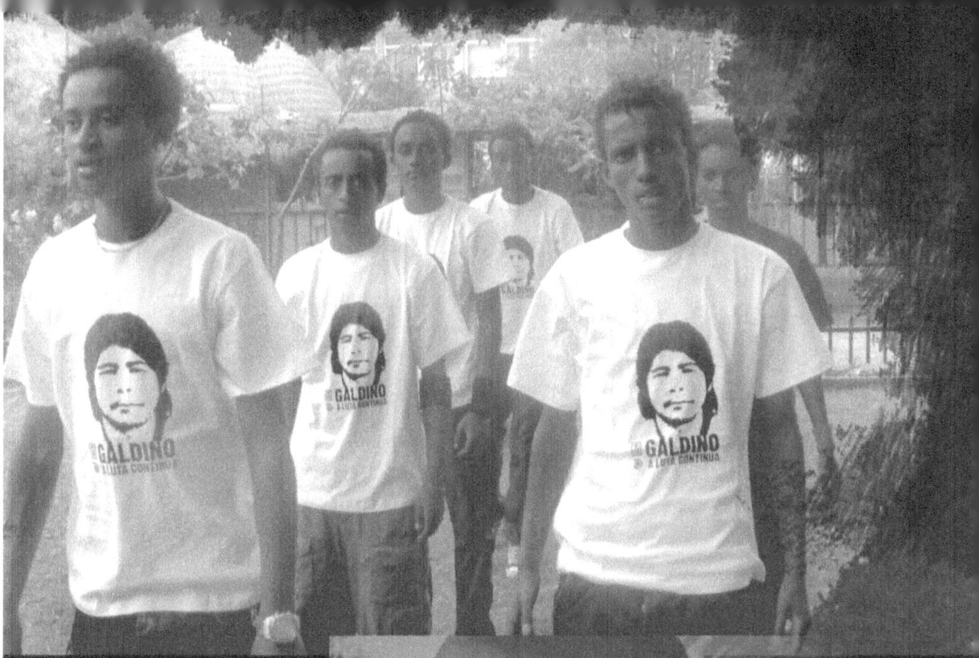

Breaks Dance Crew,
Addis Ababa, Ethiopia.

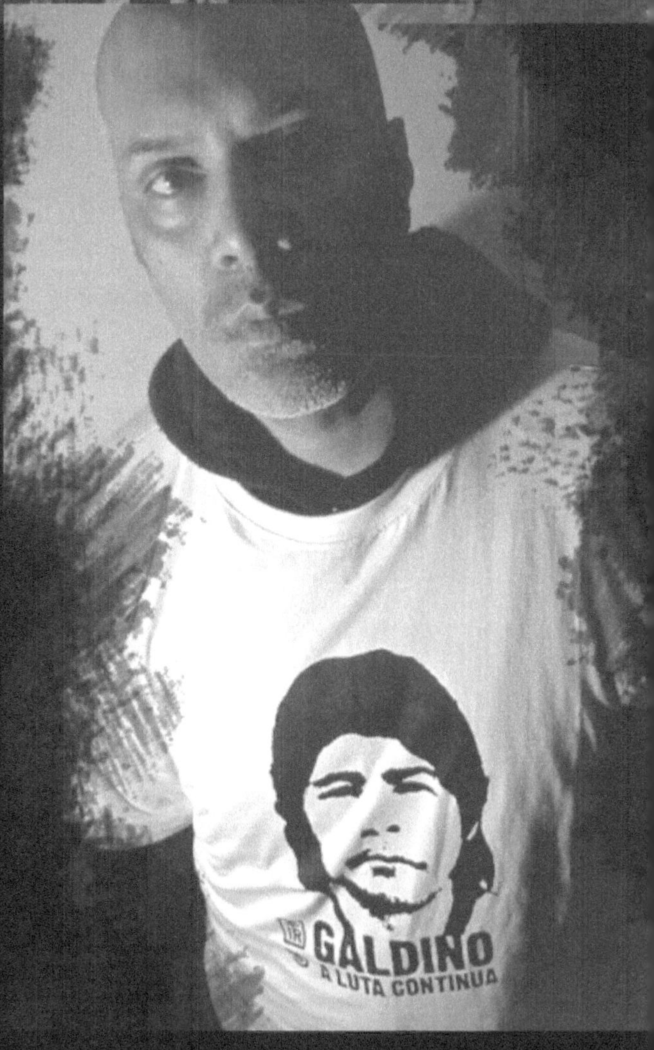

Dr. Das.
Mogelling photo
by Ramjac.

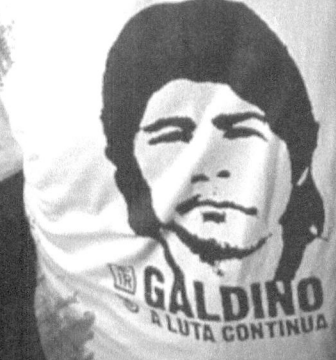

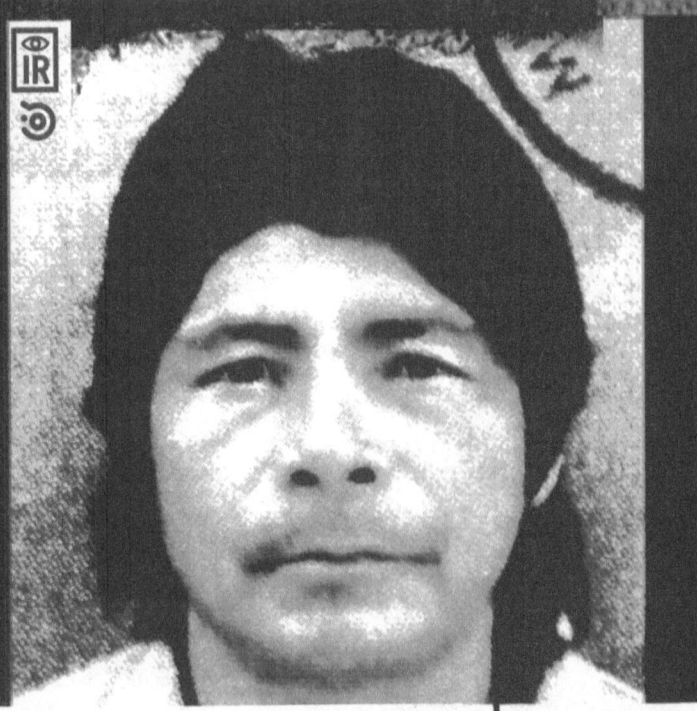

DUB FOR GALDINO

21 DE FEVEREIRO • CARAPICUÍBA • COHAB 5 • 15H

UM TRIBUTO AO SÍMBOLO DA RESISTÊNCIA INDÍGENA PT.1

DEEDER ZAMAN
ASIAN DUB FOUNDATION • REBEL UPRISING

DUBDEM SOUND SYSTEM
LABOMB..GRAFFITI AO VIVO

21/02 • COHAB 5 • MALVINA • 15H
R. BOM JARDIM DE MINAS • CARAPICUÍBA

FESTA NA RUA PRA TODOS

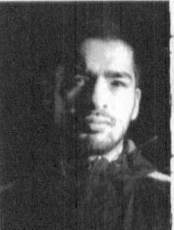

DEEDER ZAMAN: ASIAN DUB FOUNDATION • REBEL UPRISING (UK)
DUBDEM SOUND SYSTEM: SOUND SYSTEM REGGAE ESTILO JAMAICANO
INDIGENOUS RESISTANCE: UMA AÇÃO DO COLETIVO REVOLUCIONÁRIO

LANÇAMENTO DA MÚSICA
GALDINO 2010 • DEEDER ZAMAN & INDIGENOUS RESISTANCE
LA BOMB.GRAFFITI E ARRECADAÇÃO DE ALIMENTOS

dubreality.com
deederzaman.com
onusound.com

Dubdem na web:
dubdem.com.br
flickr.com/dubdem
twitter.com/dubdem
myspace.com/dubdem

Parceiros:
Débora Fidélis Produções (Audição Cultural)
& Rafael Dum Dum.
debi_fidelis@hotmail.com

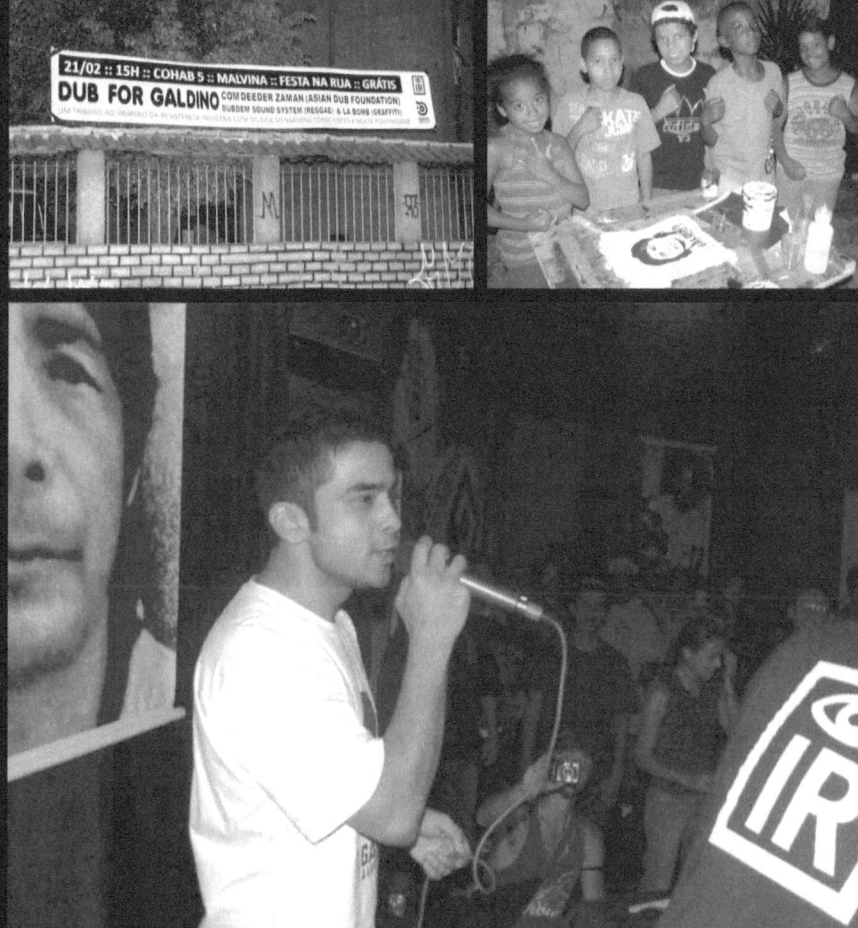

THE BLAKK INDIAN RESISTANCE

The following are three excerpts from the book **"UNDERSTANDING THE CONNECTIONS BETWEEN BLACK & ABORIGINAL PEOPLES"** written by **RAGING BLAKKINDIAN DUB** and published in 2002 by TFTT.

UNDERSTANDING THE CONNECTIONS BETWEEN
BLACK AND ABORIGINAL PEOPLES

RAGING BLAKKINDIAN DUB
The Links Between African-American, Black, Native American and Indigenous Cultures

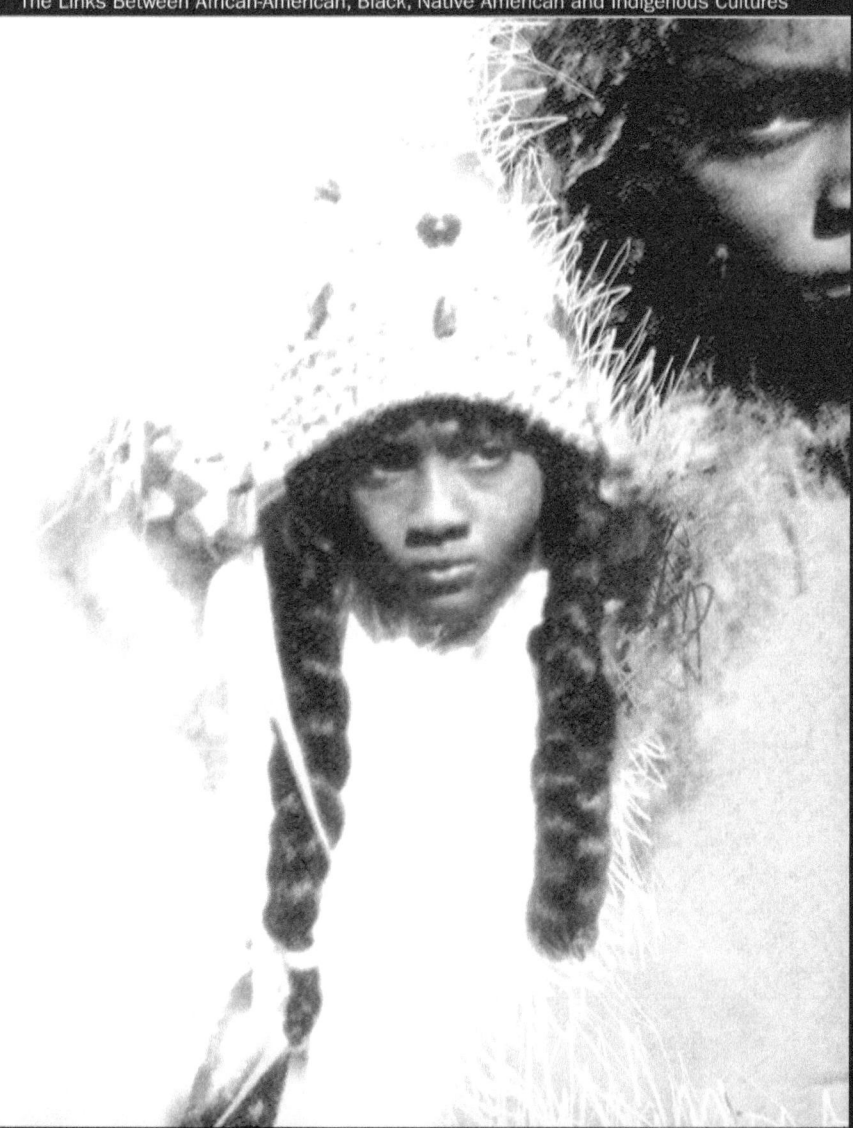

> **FOR THE OUTNUMBERED EUROPEAN COLONIALISTS, ONE OF THEIR BIGGEST FEARS WAS OF AN ALLIANCE BETWEEN AFRICAN SLAVES AND ABORIGINAL PEOPLES. THEY HAD CONCRETE EXAMPLES OF WHAT COULD HAPPEN WHEN THIS ALLIANCE OCCURRED.**

Mexico experienced its first widespread wave of slave insurrections in the period 1560-80. The Spanish colonialists had increased the number of African slaves brought into the country to work in mines and estates. By the 1560s, fugitive slaves from the northern mines were terrorizing regions from Guadalajara to Zacateca, allying with the Indians and raiding ranches. Viceroy Martin Enrique noted that in 1572 and 1574 that "cooperation between Negroes and Indians made repression all the more difficult and requested aid from Spain".

The fear of Black and Aboriginal as people is not something that is dated, it continues on today in contemporary life and politics. One of the most intriguing and certainly different spins on this fear comes from Canadian communications theorist Marshall McLuhan. In a Playboy interview during the 1960s, he stated, "the cultural aggression of white America against Negroes and Indians is not based on skin colour and belief in racial superiority, whatever ideological clothing may be used to rationalize it but on the white man's inchoate awareness that the Negro and Indian as men with deep roots in resonating tribal world are actually physically and

socially superior to the fragmented alienated and dissociated man of western civilization. Such a recognition, which stabs at the heart of the white man's entire social value system inevitably, generates violence and genocide. It has been the sad fate of the Negro and the Indian to be tribal men in a fragmented culture, men born ahead of their time".

While I feel that his opinions come from a very romanticized view of Black and Aboriginal people and I certainly don't agree with his casual dismissal of White supremacy, I do find it somewhat noteworthy that an essentially non-political but renown White scholar in his own manner is acknowledging and attempting to analyze White people's fear of Black and Aboriginal people.

I met with aboriginal author and historian Jack Forbes, who has conducted extensive research on this subject. He pointed out to me that about twenty years ago an article was published in the Journal of Negro History entitled "Divide and Rule." It detailed what was called "The South Carolina Policy." This was the colonial policy in South Carolina that was developed specifically to make Aboriginal peopes afraid of Africans and vice versa. According to Forbes, this policy was somewhat successful in that the different African rebellions were separate from the Aboriginal rebellions without the two forces helping each other. By playing one group against the other, even though they were a small minority, the whites managed to survive through this successful "divide and rule" policy.

This fear of a Black and Aboriginal alliance has also, in my opinion, manifested itself in the attempted erasure of the joint history of African and Aboriginal people. Both Jack Forbes and author Doug Sivad point to the following glaring omission in terms of recent document American history as one example of this.

> In the summer of 1526, Spanish colonialist Lucas Vasquez de Ally landed at the mouth of the Peedee River in present day South Carolina with a hundred Spaniards and one hundred African slaves from Haiti. Malaria, raids by aboriginal people and ultimately a slave revolt forced the

Spanish colonialists to flee after a short period of time. The African maroons who remained established a settlement and prospered, friendly to some aboriginal people, foes to others. Since no African women were brought during early African slavery, these Africans intermarried with Aboriginal people. This Blakk Indian settlement predates any of the other European settlements recorded in the history books, yet it is difficult to find acknowledgment of this fact.

Jack Forbes feels one of the causes for this is what he calls the "White Hub" of scholarship. Academic research has privileged Europeans, making them the centre of activity. Everyone that the Europeans have contact with is on the periphery. Consequently, scholars will examine the relationship between White people and Black people or the relationship between White people and Aboriginal people but rarely will they examine the relationship between Black people and Aboriginal people.

This kind of thinking has also permeated the minds of the general western population. In North America, I have always been puzzled by most of the discussions I've heard on the subject of "interracial marriage". Most people using this term refer to the union of a White person with another person of colour. For some reason, people discount the possibility that an interracial marriage may also refer to the union of people of colour from different racial backgrounds - Chinese and Black, for instance.

The repercussions of this kind of thinking can be easily seen by an examination of cinema. "Daughters of the Dust" by Julie Dash was the first film that I have seen which depicted a union between an African and an Aboriginal person. As Julie Dash said in an interview with bell hooks, "There are certain tribes that were absorbed within the Black community to the point where you couldn't distinguish Native American features. They just look African American. And to my knowledge that intermarrying has never been depicted on the screen,

a Native American and an African American mating, bonding creating a

life together that wasn't just built upon some lust of the moment. I wanted to show that".

There are other political ramifications that arise from the denial and attempted erasure of joint African and Aboriginal history. One of these centers around the issue of land. As Jack Forbes said to me, "White society doesn't want African Americans putting forward claims and saying yes we are part Native people, you owe us something not just for slavery, but you owe us something else because we are native people, we were here first, we have a claim to this land".

Land has always been one of the primary tools that the United States government has used to cause separation and aboriginal people. When I was in New Orleans, photographer and historian, Michael P. Smith explained to me the "Red Bone" communities were prevalent in Louisiana. These communities were created when Aboriginal people went to sign treaties with the government. The government would tell them we can't give you land since you aren't really "Indian" — there are too many Black people among you. So the Aboriginal people would return and create communities on the outskirts of their communities where they would send those among them that looked "too black." Afterwards they would return to the government and say we are only Aboriginal people living here,

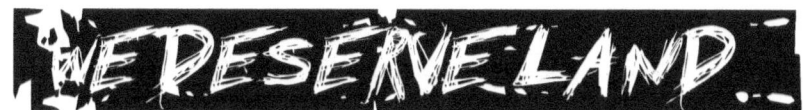

Jack Forbes also pointed out the case of the Freedman people in Oklahoma. They were citizens of various tribes in Oklahoma, who were also of African ancestry. In the 1890s, when the tribes were broken up by a government act, those who the government considered Aboriginal people by blood were given land in individual parcels that were protected by a trust status. As a consequence of their looking "too African," the Freedmen were given their land without trust protection, which generally meant that their land went on the market and whites were able to get a hold of it. By contrast, those Aboriginal people who received their land with trust protection had sale of their land restricted, which continues today.

Due to the fact that they looked "too African," the Freedmen weren't even allowed to record even their degree of Aboriginal blood, even though they were citizens of the Cree and Cherokee nations. As a result, they had no continuing legal relationship with the US government as aboriginal people. These ties were completely severed. A situation that Jack Forbes feels is a violation of treaties, a violation of law, and a potential area of litigation. Maneuvers like these by the US government were very common. When one considers for example that on the east coast of the U.S., practically every tribe is a mixture of African and First Nations one begins to understand the potential scope of litigation that could be brought by Blakk Indian people against the US government.

(Coincidentally, after I wrote this paragraph I picked up a newspaper and read that aboriginal people had put forward a claim to Ellis Island in New York. To me, this is just the tip of the iceberg of the potential land claims that could be brought against the US government).

Blakk indian children in Yungas, Bolivia.

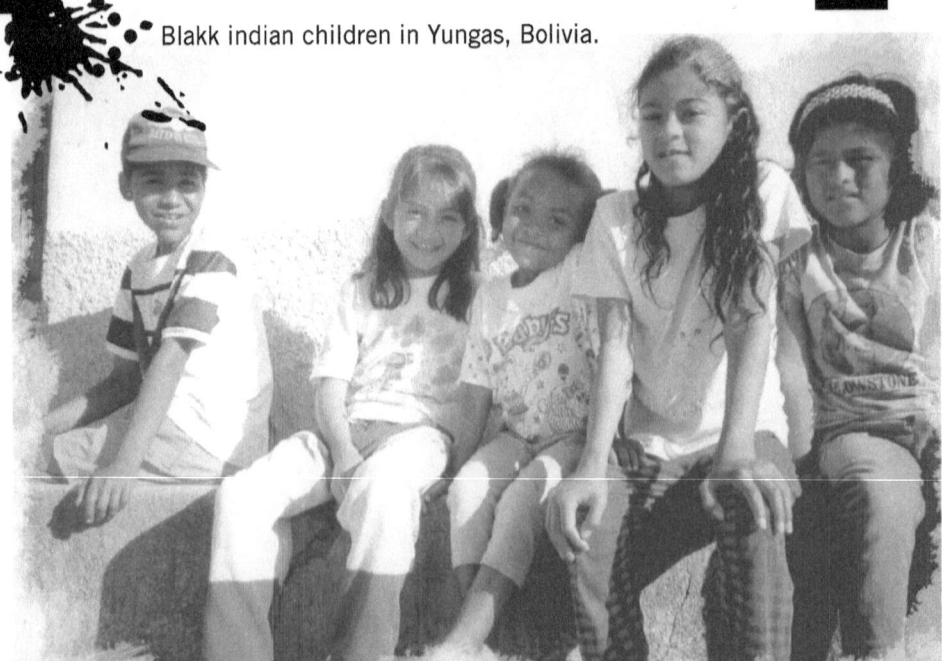

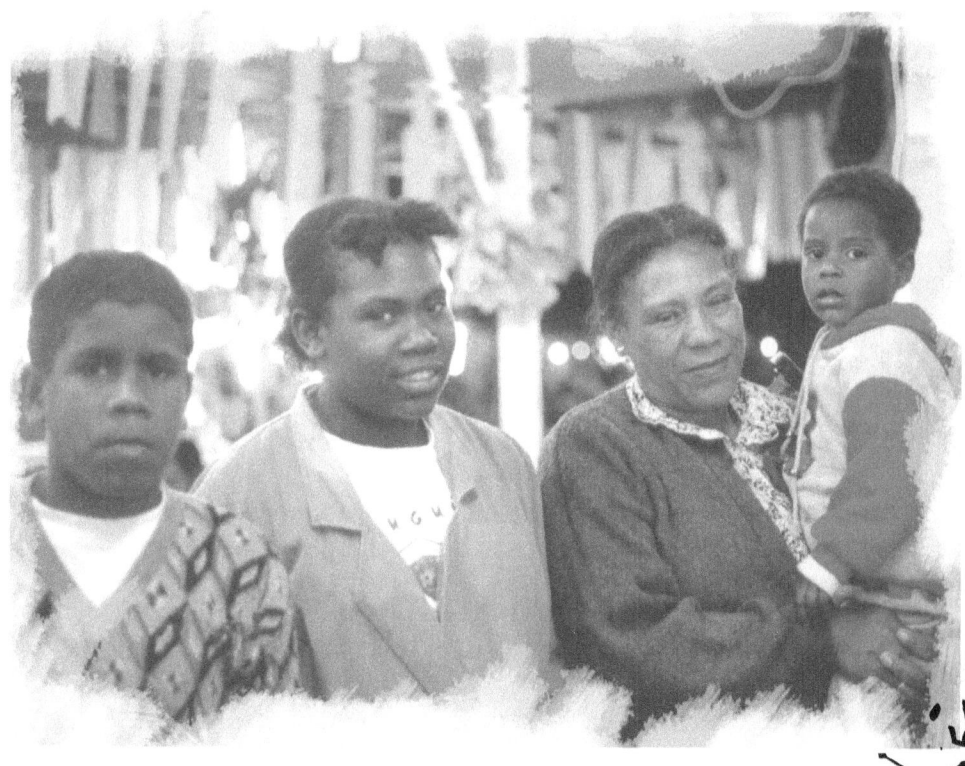

Blakk indian family in Peru.

There are some contemporary examples of the empathy Black people feel for Aboriginal people in North America. It may be this empathy that past and present settler governments have feared. Later on, I will critically examine the reality of political alliances between Black and Aboriginal people. First I would like to present some of the contemporary real life stories that have been passed on to me and which are not found in history books.

I remember sitting in the kitchen of the Vancouver home of Lee and Dennis Maracle when Lee, a prolific writer and Aboriginal activist shared these stories with me.

"We saw the empathy of Black people for Indians during the Longest Walk (An Aboriginal political march across the US). A friend of ours had to leave her car in the city — so she said I will leave it in a Black ghetto so if it gets stolen at least Black people will get it. So she parked this car, which had the "Longest Walk" bumper sticker in this ghetto and left it. Six months later, she went back to the neighbourhood and to her surprise the car was there as she left it; and all the Black people who greeted her in the neighbourhood told her that they had looked after the car for her.

Dennis had experiences of going to this school during the 1960s where there were a lot of Black and White confrontations. One day they were having a riot at the school where the Black kids were beating on these White kids in the corridor and Dennis came walking through. It was like the parting of the Red Sea — the Black kids let him walk through the fighting totally untouched because they could see that he was Indian".

One day while sitting on the lawn of the Native Friendship Centre in Toronto, I spied a friend of my brother, a Black musician named Kerwin. We started chatting away and the following conversation ensued.

"You can ask your brother from way back, I always said, you know, I'll give my sympathy to the Native people first before I give it to Black people because it's their land. My father would always show us books and films like newsreels of Malcolm X and the ones that depicted how the Indians were massacred and the buffalo slaughtered. Let me tell you something that happened in high school. It was 1973; the teacher's name was Mr. Fagen. He was our history teacher and he was always Sir Winston this and Sir Winston that, so I got up and said,

WHY DON'T YOU TELL THE WHOLE TRUTH,

what the settlers did to get this land, how they stole, how they killed the Indians. "Well, you know how White people can get really red — well, this guy turned totally red and he pointed to me and said, "You sit down!" When I sat down, he pointed to me again, his face still red and said, "You get up and get out of here. Go to the principal's office". So, I went to the principal's office where they suspended me for a week. They called my father, who was really proud of me and really angry with them. He told them, "You just want to suspend him for telling the truth". A sampling of contemporary African American rap and poetry reveals a lyrical rendering of this empathy."Take a piece of America back but who had if first hear the Indian Curse" Public Enemy How we gonna make the Black Nation rise? Remember the so-called Indian, look what they did to him — maybe they'll do that to us! " Brother D.

THE BLUES HAVE BEEN RIPPED OFF LIKE JAZZ,
ripped off like the Indians, ripped off like the land " Gil Scott Heron The Fire This Time issued their single "Oka Ain't Over" drawing the parallels between the government assault on Aboriginal people and the numerous police shootings of innocent Black people.

Whether it has been acts like raising the Aborigine flag during their Australian tours or addressing chapters of the American Indian movement, rap group Public Enemy has always been ready to support indigenous movements worldwide. Unknown to the general public is the behind scenes communications that Chuck D from Public Enemy has had with Aboriginal youth and the warriors who were involved at the standoff at Kahnesatake.

While a guest on the Canadian literary television show "Imprint," Harry Allen, Public Enemy's "media assassin" threw a lot of the listening public totally off guard when he accepted a welcome from the host Daniel Richler by stating, "thanks for having me on your stolen land." Later on the show, he caused further consternation when addressing the issue of white racism he raised concerns of both Black and aboriginal people. While this confounded those who expected him to be "pro-black" and only address "Black" concerns, his comments were enthusiastically greeted by Aboriginal and Blakk Indian people watching the show. In fact, his comments formed the foundation for The Fire This Time track "Basslines and Ballistics".

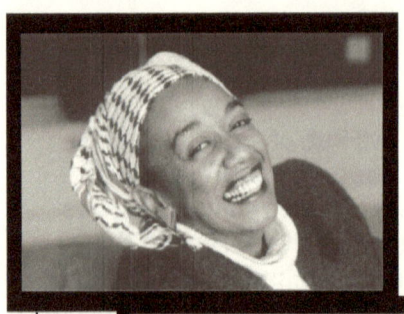
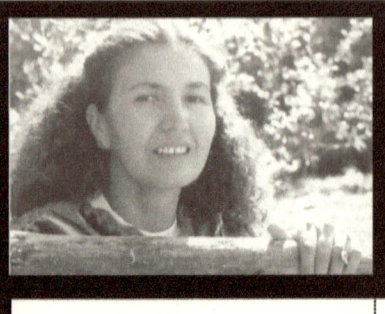
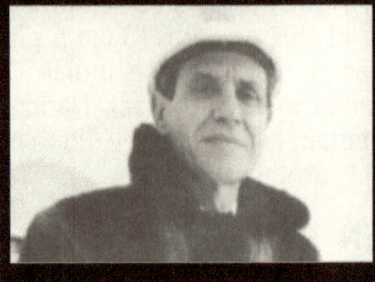

Dub poet Binta Breeze, on a Canadian tour, continued to speak out about the injustice facing aboriginal people in Canada despite the torrent of criticism she received from raising the issue. One of the most moving and profound demonstrations of support for Aboriginal people that I have witnessed occurred at a Fugees, Ben Harper and Spearhead concert at the Opera House in Toronto in 1993. This was a year when rap was under violent attack by the media who were intent on categorizing it as violent and sexist. After a moving performance by Ben Harper (who is another artist of Blakk Indian ancestry) and the Innocent Criminals, headliners Spearhead took to the stage. Earlier that evening I had given Spearhead founder Michael Franti a copy of the book of aboriginal philosophy, The Native Creative Process, by Jeannette Armstrong and Douglas Cardinal.

Franti and another member of the band began their show by stating that they first had to show respect for the aboriginal people's whose land they were on. Myself and many in the audience were both surprised and touched when he then read a passage of Native philosophy to the hushed capacity audience, who responded with huge applause. The group then performed their piece "Of Course You Can," which contains the refrain, "One day the indigenous people of this earth are going to reclaim the land that is rightfully theirs".

As a footnote, a few years later, I was walking in downtown Toronto and ended up in conversation with some young Aboriginal street kids. One of them was listening to some music on his Walkman. I asked him what he was listening to. "Spearhead," he replied. "I was at a concert a while back and this group came out and paid respect to my people and I have been listening to them ever since".

I wish to make it clear that by no means do I consider the aforementioned stories to be the full sum of acts by musicians and poets in support of Aboriginal people. There are many, many more. However, these just happen to be the ones that I've been privy to and wish to share.

Travelling through North America in the late 1980s, I had the opportunity to meet with two women, one African American, the other Aboriginal. Both had been influenced by political and spiritual thought from each other's culture to the point that they had transformed their lives and dedicated it to these principles. I had been hitchhiking in Arizona and New Mexico with my destination being the Navajo Nation Fair in New Mexico where my friend John Williams and his all-aboriginal reggae band "Native Roots" were going to be playing. I had arrived at the Navajo Nation Fair in a torrential thunderstorm. Sloshing through the mud trying to find the concert site, I noticed this white van that was parked on the fair ground. It was covered with a beautiful painting of

Bob Marley, Malcolm X, Peter Tosh and Marcus Garvey.

As well, in huge red, gold, and green lettering it also said "Stop Police Violence" and "How Can You Call the Cops on Cops!". Soon I was talking with the owner of the van, a Navajo woman named Cimi Boone. She was selling medicinal herbs and T-shirts that had a picture of Bob Marley on it with the caption "How Can You Call the Cops on the Cops". Not surprisingly, the police had hassled her entering the fairground with her van.

Cimi had been inspired by the words of Bob Marley, Peter Tosh, Malcolm X, Marcus Garvey and Martin Luther King. She now identified herself as a Rastafarian as she felt there were so many things within the Rastafarian beliefs, which were in tune with her Aboriginal beliefs.

Following the example of Black radicals, she had devoted her life to **fighting the system** and trying to live outside of it as much as possible. She had helped organize a group, which fought against police violence. This group was a coalition of Aboriginal, Black, Latino and White people who had been harassed and brutalized by the police. Part of their campaign was to draw attention to the fact there was no mechanism to address the wrong doing of the police — hence the T-shirt with the caption "How Can You Call the Cops on the Cops".

Now she was living in her van travelling to different First Nations communities with information about people like Marcus Garvey and Bob Marley as well as literature about the campaign against police brutality.

She had given birth to her son at home and had purposely not registered him at the hospital or with the social security system. She had done this because she didn't want the "Babylonian" system to have any knowledge of his existence. This would further facilitate his remaining outside of the system.

In Vancouver, Canada, my friend Farah Shroff introduced me to Dale Edwards. An African American now living in Vancouver, she dedicates her life to activism in support of Aboriginal people. She had been particularly inspired by the political philosophy of George Manuel, an Aboriginal political figure from the Shuswap nation. George Manuel's philosophy of being self-sufficient also led her to change specific areas in the way she lived her life. From Aboriginal people in Mount Currie she learnt various skills on how to live off the land so she could be less dependent on needing money from the system to survive.

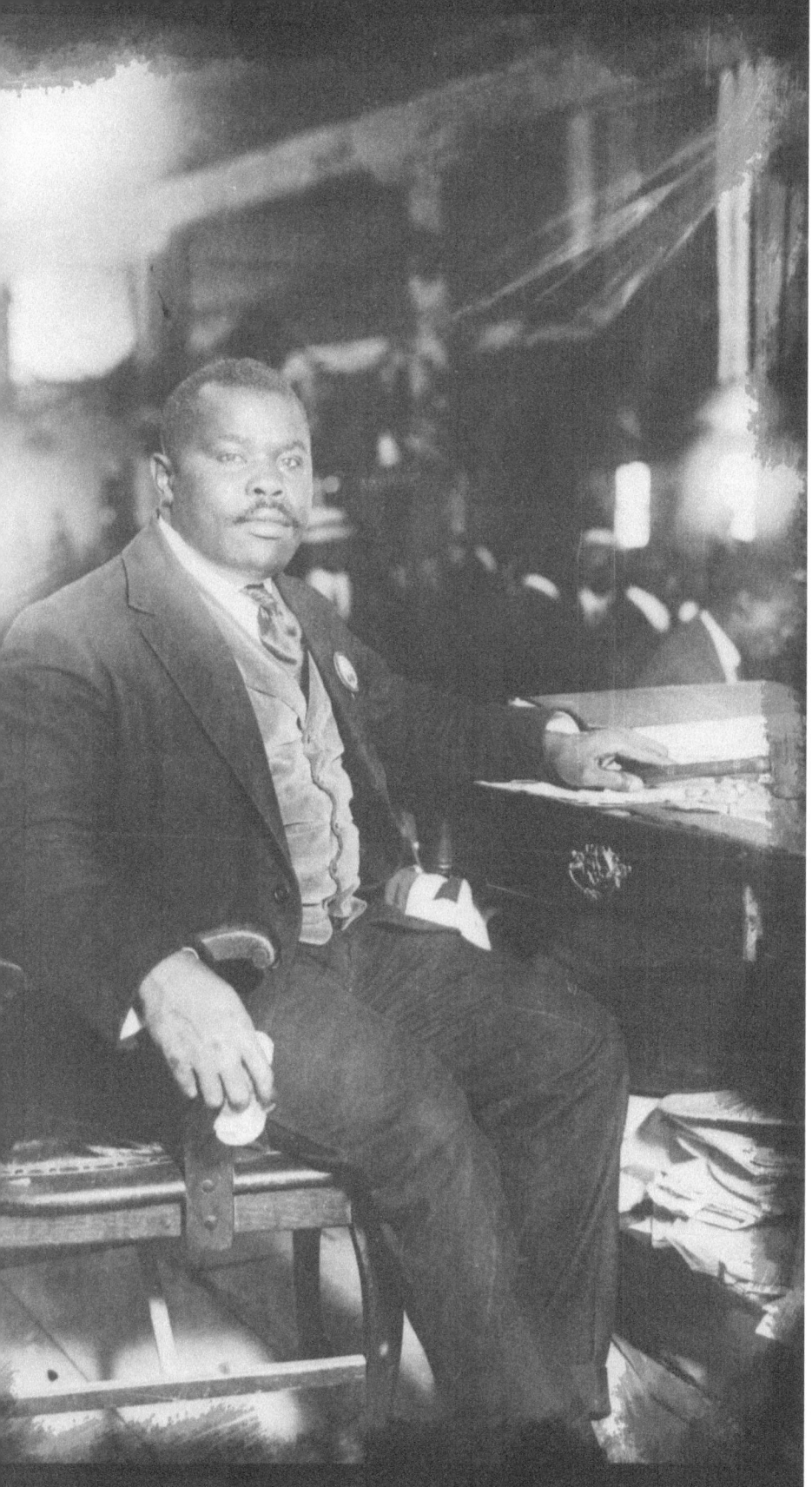

I spoke to George Manuel in 1985. Even though he was ill and confined to a wheel chair at the time, he was still a fiery and inspiring orator. He was still feared by the Canadian settler government, as indicated by the RCMP officers that I observed monitoring him. Throughout his life, Manuel had drawn the ire of the Canadian settler government. Not only did he work and strategize towards a unified Aboriginal political force in Canada, but also he was especially visionary in the manner in which he strategized and examined the situation of indigenous peoples all over the world. It was George Manuel who coined the phrase "fourth world" to refer to the collective state of indigenous people around the world. He traveled extensively throughout South and Central America visiting indigenous communities as well as to Africa where he met with and was inspired by the policies of Tanzanian's then-president Julius Nyerere. While he worked in the Canadian city of Ottawa, he frequently met with African diplomats who were also working there. George explained to me the strategies and experiences of African peoples in their fight against colonialism was something that had been very important to him. This influence can be seen in an excerpt from an address he made to an aboriginal political organization. **"THE AFRICAN SUBJUGATED PEOPLE CRY OUT FOR UHURU · FREEDOM",** he wrote. "The Indian people should cry out both for UHURU and unity for it is only through unity that we will have real freedom."

While there exists many more acts of Black and Aboriginal political solidarity, I feel at the same time it is essential not to romanticize the reality of this alliance. It's also necessary to try and clearly put into perspective the significance and potential benefits of this alliance. A successful alliance requires a solid foundation built on mutual respect and understanding of the similarities and differences in perspectives and agendas of the groups involved.

Various forces such as colonialism, miseducation, different historical and spiritual experiences and practices have prevented black and aboriginal people from completely understanding each other's political perspectives and agendas. It has also been difficult to access accurate accounts of each other's histories and philosophies.

Many Black and Aboriginal people have understood the need to address this by owning and controlling their own educational and information resources. From my perspective, understanding the links between Black and Aboriginal struggles is of utmost importance. However, **so is the need to always keep in mind the larger political picture within which all struggles occur. The importance of this approach becomes apparent as one observes Black and Aboriginal people who decide to support the destructive forces of capitalism and state power.**

All over the world, among situations of great poverty, there is always Aboriginal or Black elite who plays their part in the process of exploitation.

CRITICAL ANALYSIS OF STATE STRUCTURES AND STATE POWER IS VITAL. ANARCHIST THOUGHT AND PRACTICES · WHICH HAS NUMEROUS PRECEDENTS WITHIN BLACK AND ABORIGINAL CULTURES · HAS MADE A VALUABLE CONTRIBUTION IN THIS REGARD.

Books like "African Anarchism the History of a Movement" by Sam Mbah and I. E Igariwey (See Sharp Press 1997) provide important details about these anarchist traditions.
One of the values of Black and Aboriginal peoples having a better understanding of each others cultures and histories is the potential strengthening and enrichment that can occur from them having contact with one another.

Black psychotherapist Bob Manning is an example of how this can occur. After being exposed to traditional aboriginal healing practices, he was able to incorporate this knowledge into his healing methods and consequently provide more effective counseling for street kids.

Some Black and Aboriginal people have drawn upon their respective historical experiences and philosophies to come up with radical political analysis. When these various analyses are combined, they have the ability to improve the tools that can be used for radical analysis. The benefits of a combined Black and Aboriginal political analysis obviously have the potential to benefit more than just Black and Aboriginal people. The possibilities of how this can occur is vividly illustrated by an essay "The Need For Alternatives in understanding The Struggle of the Lubicon Lake Cree", by SumitaBidaye, a writer of South Asian decent. In this essay, she is able to overcome the shortcomings of radical eco philosophies in being able to analyse the situation facing the Lubicon Lake Cree. She does this by utilising the philosophy and political analysis of Black activist and MOVE founder John Africa combined with analysis provided by the American Indian Movement. From her viewpoint, radical eco philosophies are unable to adequately address the role of colonialism in the case of the Lubicon Lake Cree. By drawing on the analysis provided by Black and Aboriginal people who have been directly affected by colonial domination and genocide, she is able to provide more that the usual conclusion of "environmental injustice" that is arrived at by environmentalists.

This is just one example of how Blakk Indian political philosophies can advance political struggle.

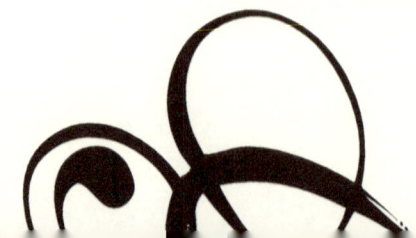

BLACK PANTHER
for Self-Defe[nse]

"THERE ARE NO LAWS THAT THE OPPRESSOR MAKES THAT THE OPPRESSED ARE BOUND TO RESPECT"

HUEY P. NEWTON

murdered Aug 22 1989

EXPLORING SPIRITUAL CONNECTIONS

A common point that doesn't seem to have provoked much dispute is the fact that Africans and Aboriginal people, upon first contact, discovered that they shared a spiritual outlook that had many parallels. Certainly key to this was the shared belief in the spirit world. I remember vividly one of the first conversations that I had with Jeannette Armstrong, Okanagan Indian writer and educator, when she said to me, "they try to tell us the spirit world doesn't exist, that the spirits don't exist,

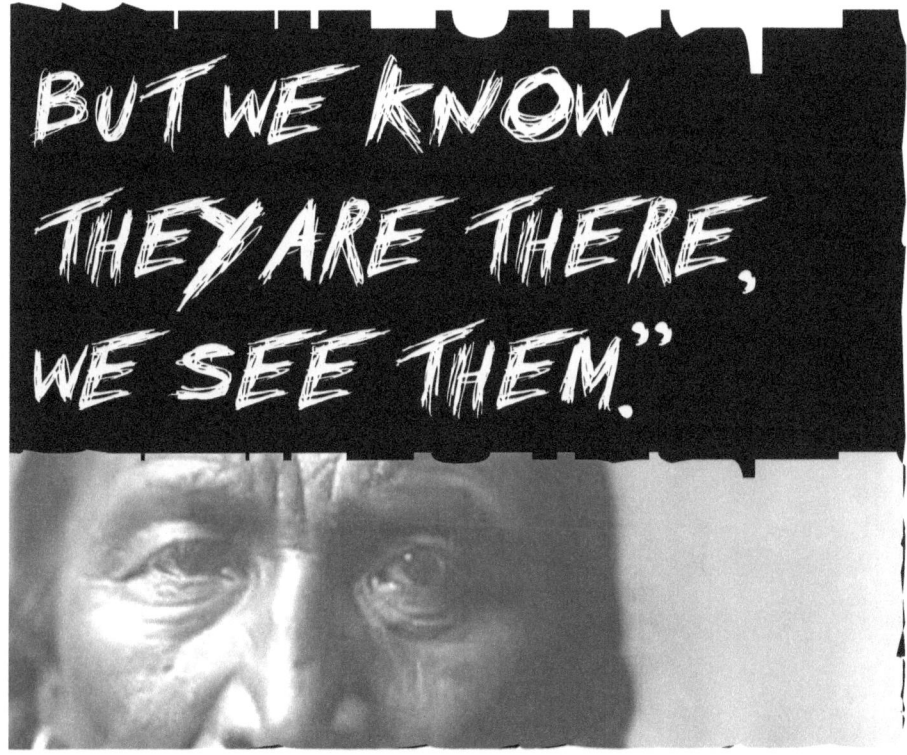

BUT WE KNOW THEY ARE THERE, WE SEE THEM."

This mutual recognition of the spirit world by some Black and Aboriginal people was brought home to me in an episode that was recounted to me years ago. An Aboriginal activist had been jailed and his immediate family was worried about him. They consulted a medicine person, who transformed into a coyote and appeared in the prison to see what was occurring with this

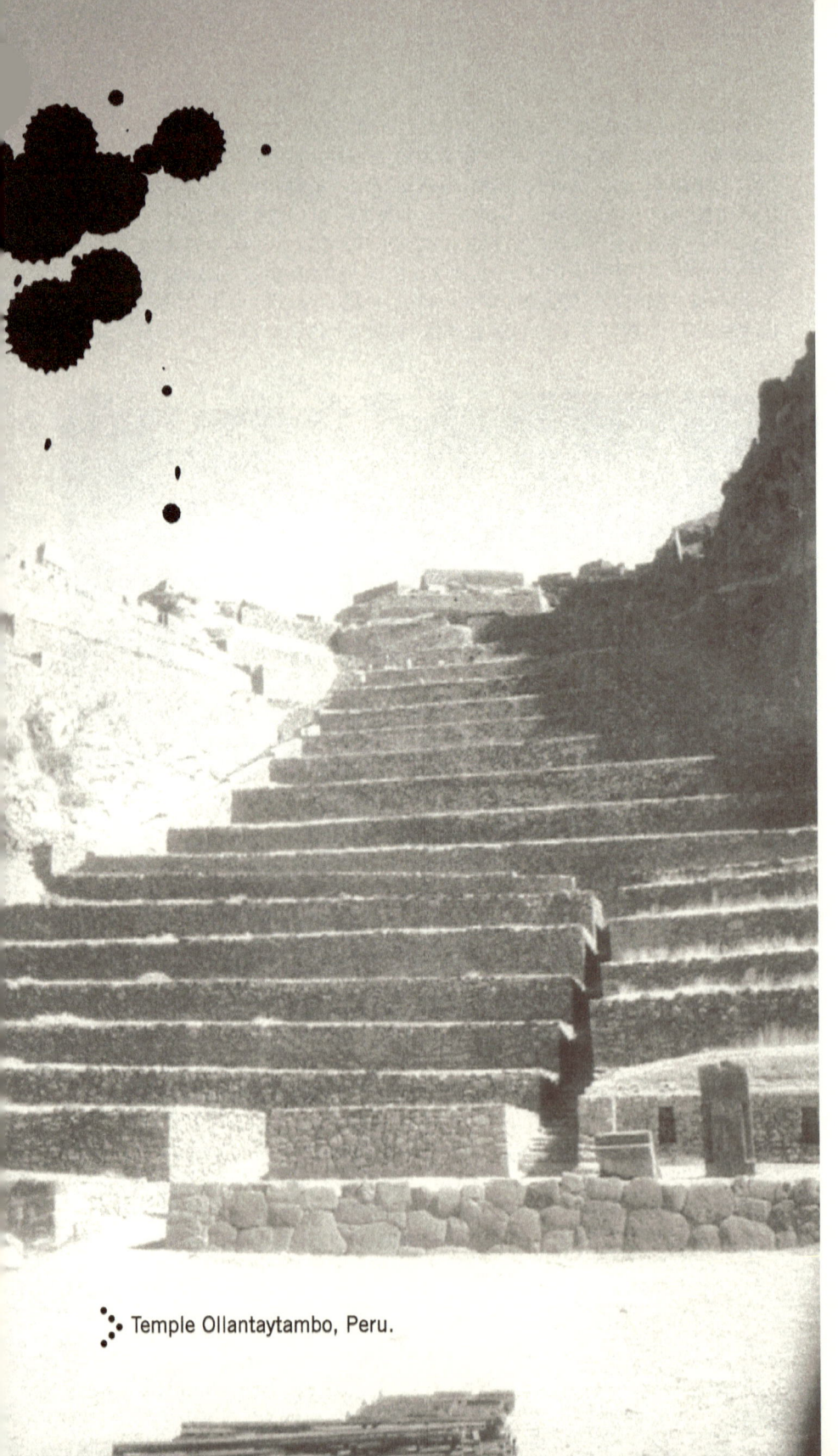
Temple Ollantaytambo, Peru.

family member. According to the activist, when the coyote appeared, it was as if time was frozen momentarily and then the coyote disappeared. It happened to be suppertime when this occurred, even though numerous inmates were around at the time, not one of them saw or commented on the appearance of the coyote. However, the Aboriginal activist said right afterwards a sole Black inmate approached him with a scared look in his eyes and said, "did you see that coyote?". Talking with him further, he discovered that this inmate's grandmother practiced a traditional African religion.

Intrigued by this event, and pondering its significance; I went and visited with my close friend Pineshi Gustin, who is a keeper of traditional Ojibway ways. I recounted the episode to her and she had the following response for me:

"As a child, I learnt from the elders that we are born in the world but the realities are not split off like we would think. They believe the spirit world and this world are in sync, that there is no separation —so when that incident happened to your friend and this other Black guy, they were operating on the same level and they tuned out the reality as it exists right now —this dense thing —and slip into the spirit world —but it's still there — there's no separation —it happens simultaneously with what's happening around us right now and then they slip right back out.

On Turtle Island some people especially white people are being programmed not to live in the spirit world. Somewhere in their psyche they have been programmed to be mass orientated, to control of the mind, which is the weakest control of all —the powerful control sits in the spirit. If someone with this mindset were in front of me now as I went into the spirit world I would loose him or her —but I know I can sit here and go quickly into that world without loosing you because of your spiritual orientation.

So I do relate to the story of these two simultaneously seeing the coyote because that coyote did exist. That part of native people does exist. I would not say it's lost because it exists on its own".

Shared belief in the spirit world was just one of several ties Black and Aboriginals found they had in common. Similar worldviews in regards to nature and ancestral spirits were also present. One of my particular areas of interest is in locating examples of what occurred with one another.

Chilean visual artist Andrea offers a perceptive insight into the investigation of possible syncretic beliefs. It is her view that altars are one of the best indicators of syncretic belief systems since altars contain representations of and offerings to important spiritual deities. Altars are thus important reflections of the spiritual cosmology of a people.

A look at altars in Brasil (named peij) that are used in the Umbanda religion and in African spiritualists churches in New Orleans (U.S.A) bear out this observation. The peijs in Brasil not only have representations of traditional African deities but also Aboriginal deities that are indigenous to the area. This bears witness to the fact that the Umbanda religion combines elements of both African and Aboriginal spirituality.

If one visits African Spiritualist Churches in New Orleans, not only will one find altars that will have offering to African saints but you will also find statues of Chief Black Hawk. Black hawk, who was a Sauk and Fox warrior who led a heroic resistance against the US government in the 1800 's. He is worshipped as a symbol of peace and justice in African Spiritualist churches. In Louisiana, his spirit, along with other Aboriginal spirits like White Hawk are summoned in the course of worship to bring healing to those that need it.

During the course of my travels in Cuba, especially in the city of Santiago, I witnessed altars for the Santeria religion that had statues of Aboriginal figures, it was explained to me that they were for purposes of protection. Even though presently the exact origins of Aboriginal presence in Santeria ceremonies haven't been formally explored, an examination of Cuban history does provide some potential clues. Like numerous places in the

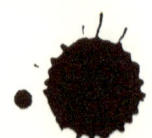

Americas, there were joint slave and Aboriginal rebellions. Contrary to the popular mythology that the indigenous Arawaks were completely exterminated , there are today still living in the Yatcras region of a few hundred miles from Santiago hundreds of descendants of Arawak Indians. Not only do they presently live separately in their own settlements but also there are Arawaks who live among the general Cuban population. Consequently, it is not farfetched to suggest that Arawak interaction with African people has resulted in syncretic beliefs.

There are other indicators other than altars that point to the possibility that African and Aboriginal interaction affect their respective spiritual practices. In Haitian voodoo practices Veve drawing of intricate designs in cornmeal is one aspect of voodoo that researchers haven't designated an African origin to. Anthropologist Maya Dereen felt that the designs were very similar to intricate Aztec and other Indians, who originally inhabited Haiti, were seafaring people who had contact with the Mayans and Aztecs.

Haitian voodoo group Boukman Esperyans had some perceptive observations on this connection. Band member Lolo in an interview with Errol Nazareth describes voodoo as not only an African religion but as an "Afro Indian religion" where the African spirit meets with the native spirit. Lolo also notes that the Haitian revolutionary Boukman united Africans and Natives to fight the French colonists in the 18 th century. He also makes the following comment "Africans and Indians see the world in the same way as we both see a parallel between the visible and the invisible world.

There are also other areas as yet to be fully explored areas of possible syncretic spiritual beliefs. One of these is the connection between the Muslim religion and the traditional Aboriginal belief.

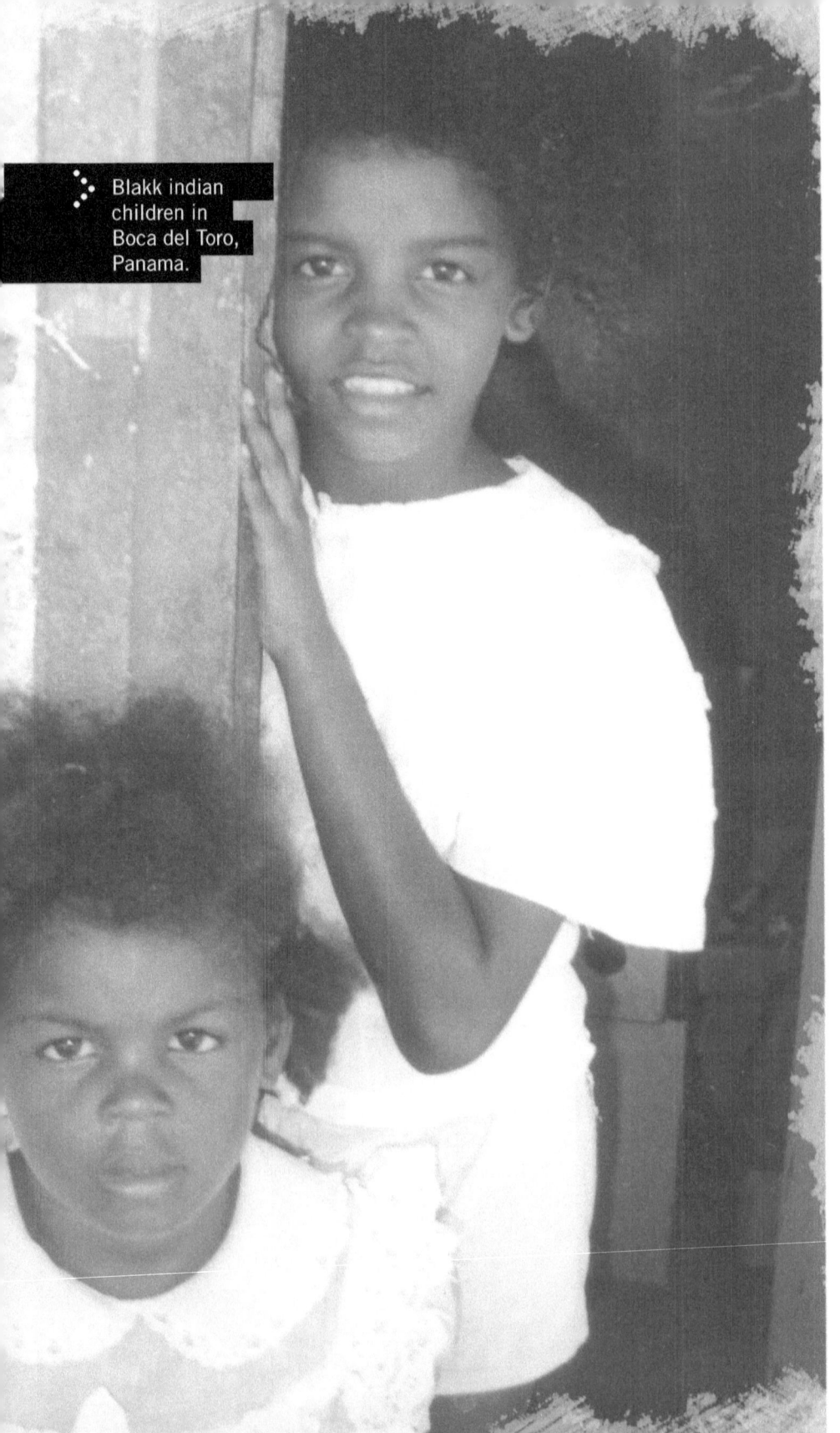

Blakk indian children in Boca del Toro, Panama.

Aboriginal Muslim researchers and activists such as Sr Maria Adin, Imman Benjamir Perez Mahomat and Br Mahirabdur Razzag are involved in investigating the spread of Islam among Aboriginal people over the last couple of centuries.

African Muslims explorers are believed to have traveled to North America centuries before Columbus; often they intermarried with Aboriginal people and never returned to Africa. This social interaction between Aboriginal and Muslims continued during the centuries of the trans Atlantic slave trade. As indicated in the July 1996 edition of the Muslim magazine "The Message", the fact that escaped African slaves joined the ranks of the Seminole Indians is not a secret. However, a previously undocumented fact was the existence and influence of African Muslim slaves who joined the Seminoles in the 1800's with men wearing Muslin styled turbans and knee length or longer shirts. For ceremonial occasions the Seminoles wore ankle length turkey feather robes. Both the Cherokees and the Seminoles routinely covered their bodies in typically Muslin fashion.

What exactly occurred when Muslim and Aboriginal spiritual beliefs encountered each other raises some very key questions. I discussed this with John Beaubien, an Aboriginal linguist of Mohawk ancestry who at one time used to attend Nation of Islam meetings. One of the immediate queries that he had was that he was be curious to know which Aboriginal traditional practices would be considered shirk (pagan) by African Muslims. For instance how would Muslims react to such things as the use of clan symbols or the belief in spirit helpers? Would these be considered shirk? We were both intrigued when we read and article by an Aboriginal Muslim who was also a pipe carrier who attended sweats. Again we both had questions about how the two belief systems coexisted now and in the past. For instance the Cherokee

WOMEN FOUGHT AS WARRIORS IN MANY BATTLES, WHAT HAVE BEEN THE REACTION OF AFRICAN MUSLIMS TO THIS?

In addition to the Muslin/Cherokee/Seminole connection there is also the possible Muslin/Aboriginal/connection within the North American nomadic tribe of Ben Ishmael, a people who were a mix of African, white and Aboriginal people. Many of the families of the tribe of Ben Ishamel have Muslim names. This possible connection is also not limited to the North American continent. During the 16 th century, the Puerto Rico sent urgent communiqués to the Spanish government about the unrest that African slaves, specifically African Muslims, were creating on the island where they escaped and joined forces with the Aboriginal inhabitants.

Besides the obvious need for further scrutiny into Aboriginal and Muslim interaction, there are other areas that also warrant investigation. As evidence continues to accumulate indicating contact between African and Mayans and Olmecas, one wonders how culture's spiritual beliefs affected each other.

While it is important that we probe the past, there are contemporary links between various Black and Aboriginal spiritual beliefs I wish to examine.

An important and very sensitive area to explore is the increasing number of Black people who are utilizing Aboriginal traditional beliefs especially for the purposes of healing. I have reasoned with many Black people who have been aided by traditional Aboriginal spiritual practices such as the sweat. In an era when spirituality is viewed by many as another commodity to be purchased and where currently there are people like Lyn Andrews, who are willing to distort and manipulate spiritual practices to cater to these consumers; it is very important to present a viewpoint which adds an important dimension in terms of explaining the scenario.

Bob Manning is a Black psychotherapist, who among other things utilizes Aboriginal practices in his work counseling street kids, many of whom are Black. His success with using Aboriginal spiritual practices with Black youth is very revealing, especially in terms of the questions it brings up in regards to the Black psyche.

For the purpose of ensuring accuracy and complete context for this topic I am presenting a transcript of my conversation with Bob Manning.

B.M I took some kids, some who were Black and who identified themselves as gay. Some white children, guys and girls who were involved in prostitution along with some gay white children and hooked them up with some macho Aboriginal kids. Then we took them down to La Pushe, dropped them off at this beach and told them they had to live together. It was a three- day retreat so we got tents and they backpacked down and I made sure they couldn't get out. It didn't work well at first. The straight kids were uptight at the gay kids and they hated each other and fought back and forth. Then one of the guys from the Indian center said we are going to do a talking circle. I wasn't sure how some of the kids were going to react. What happened that night was that the person who led the talking circle did a ceremony. He called it a council of people and what it is, was burning sage and cleaning yourself and getting rid of the negatives and bringing in the positives -each person cleansed himself. I expected some giggles from the kids that night but there wasn't and all of a sudden all this energy started focusing on this group that was on the beach at night time by this fire, under the moonlight - we went around to each person and smudged them and after that we all sat down and he said that he was going to pass an eagle feather to each person and they could talk about anything they wanted for as long as they wanted to talk. He didn't set any one about what to talk about - but everyone had to listen. No one could talk or interrupt, then the feather went from person to person after they were done - then they said all my relations and passed the eagle feather. When they said "all my relations" it meant that they were related to everything and everybody. Even though there was no theme that was stressed everyone talked about their pain and what was wrong with them and what they had gone through in their lives and each child heard that with other.

They started becoming a community. They found that they had common pains, common issues and there were tears. It started when the sun went down and went on till almost the next morning and there were only forty people there. It was very powerful that night. I had been working all over the place: Chicago, New York, Los Angeles but I had never seen anything like this. We would take kids away for 3-day retreats and we would do the talking circle. More and more black kids were coming to these retreats and more Black children started feeling and sharing on a spiritual level what was happening in the talking circles. I was wondering why were Black children being pulled more into this. The feedback I was getting from the kids was that the talking circles were connecting them with the spirituality they felt they weren't receiving in religious institutions like the Baptist Church.

MY FEELING IS THAT THE BLACK MAN, THE BLACK WOMAN OR BLACK CHILDREN HAVE NOT YET GONE THROUGH THE GRIEVING PROCESS SPIRITUALITY IN THE US AND CANADA.

D: What is the grieving process?

B: Say for instance your mother was hit in a car accident - the first thing you might feel was shock - then you might feel anger and you have to work through that and people do that in different ways and with different processes. People can get stuck in the anger then there's fear, there's depression, there's more anger - if people can go through these levels of emotions and find a resolution then they can move onto the next stage, which is healing themselves and letting go. This is what I'm saying that Black people haven't been able to work through the processes, yet because the political and spiritual atmosphere of the US and Canada isn't giving them the chance to do that. I think the Baptist church, the Catholic church and Christianity has kept people from really going through the final part of the grieving process - we have gone through all these other things - that is why when something happens there are all these riots that take place, that's the anger part of the grieving process that hasn't yet come out - that is my feeling. If you look at the grieving process you realize that there hasn't been reconciliation. When Malcolm X started talking about this it freaked a lot of people out because the next step of grieving is to recognize and start talking about it - Malcolm was saying I have to drop my last name, because of slavery. He was recognizing the problem in order to the grieving. We have to resolve the grief.

So a lot of us have turned to Aboriginal spirituality because it is the closest thing that we find helps us with these issues. The church might bring it out for us, however you are still reinserting a non-spiritual thing for something you want, which is spiritual so you will never get past a certain level. So I think sisters and brothers who are finding Native spirituality and discovering things through are really starting to break through the grieving process.

D: I was just having this interesting conversation with Ida Johns who is an Aboriginal of Coast Salish ancestry and one of the things we were talking about was I feel that on a psychic level, people of African descent living in North America are still trying to deal with that forced dislocation from Africa and that on a certain level we are in a state of disconnectedness from the earth here -this particular location we find ourselves in. This is not something that is really recognized and one of my observations is that it contains certain elements that begin to address the needs of Black people.

B.M. I agree with that - it's what I say is part of the grieving process and healing. Also, I think a lot of the symbols and elements are similar to what was used in Africa for healing purposes.

I think Black people are constantly looking for some element of spirituality. I really feel that the elements of Aboriginal people bring to us are very similar to elements that we need for our own healing process but it will never be the ultimate element that we need to find ourselves.

Interestingly, Aboriginal writer Jack Forbes in his book "Columbus and other Cannibals" had a parallel critique of Black Christianity. He feels that often-organized black sects lend themselves to dogmatism, narrowness and a concern with the petty and superficial. Black Christians would do well to look to their African Native origins instead of being dominated solely by the theology of their

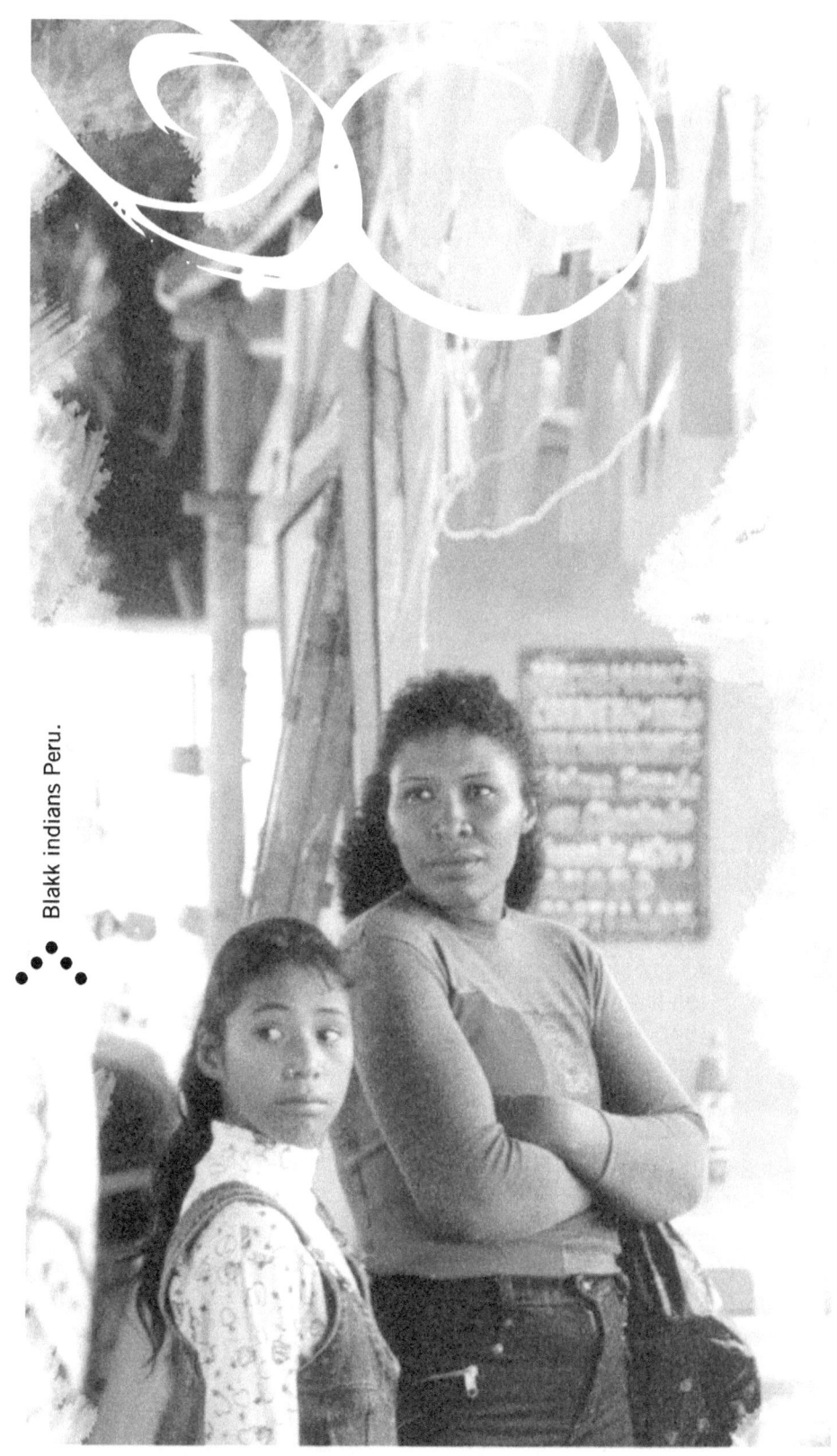
Blakk indians Peru.

European oppressor. Thus this is what a lot of Black people have been intuitively doing!! Consequently, it is also not surprising the Rastafarian spirituality with its African orientation has also been very sympathetic to Aboriginal people as well as serving as inspiration to them.

Rastafarians like Mutaburaka have deep respect for Aboriginal spirituality. I was provided with a graphic illustration of this one night after reasoning with Mutaburaka on his midnight radio show "The Cutting Edge." During our discussion about Aboriginal people Mutaburaka spontaneously pulled out a book and read part of Chief Seattle's famous speech where he among things explains why the land is not for sale and the relationship between the creator and nature.

> Readers should know that in Jamaica "The Cutting Edge" is regarded by many including myself as the best "university" in Jamaica. Everyone especially young people in the ghettos stay up during the weekday night listen to the reasoning on the show.

The next day after my appearance on the show, I was walking down a road in a small country village. Stopping by a food stand for some fruit, I over heard a Rastafarian elder talking about last nights "Cutting Edge" show. He remarked that the thing that moved him the most was to hear the speech by the "Indian Chief". To my amazement, he had written part of it down and began reciting it. This person had no idea that I was the guest on the show and this incident has stuck in my mind as an illustration of how aboriginal and Rastafarian spiritual sentiments can be in sync with one another.

Dub poet Oku Onura said the following to me while we were talking about our experiences at Aboriginal ceremonies.

"I heard their singing and chanting and it reminded me of being at a nyabingi (A Rastafarian spiritual gathering.) They are like Rasta – they are earth people.

They are like us they sit and watch –

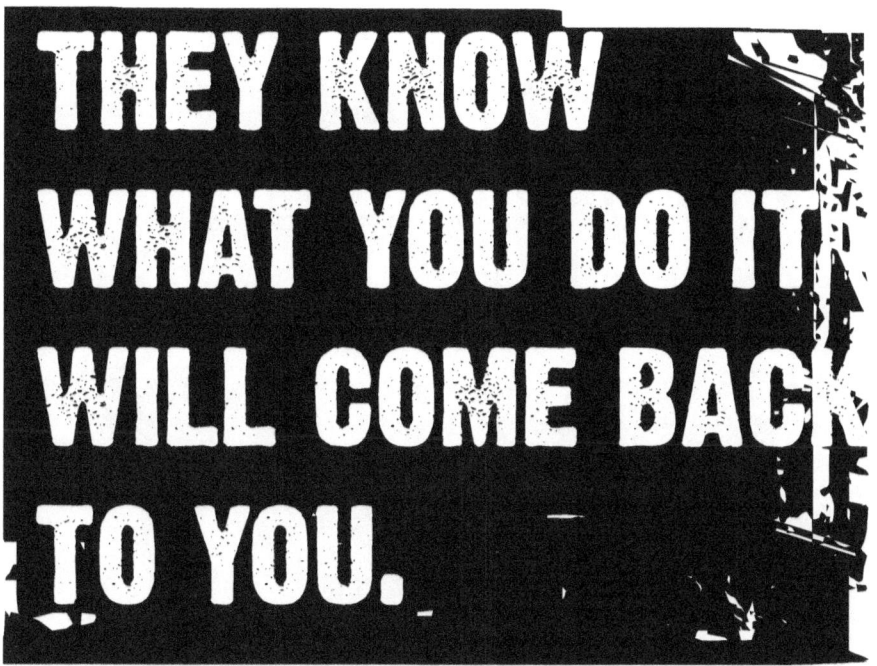

So when they look at New York they think like we do that it's heading for destruction because that's the natural order of the earth".

POSTSCRIPT

This original article was written more than ten years. So many things/many evolutions have happened since. Too many to write at this moment. However a couple of minutes ago i saw something that moved me to write this postscript. I have just finished watching what I considered a brillant talk by Jamaican Rastafarian: Mutaburaka. He spoke about how Rastafari is an evolution, constantly evolving and that his own understanding of Rastafari had evolved

"RASTAFARI IS NOT ABOUT WORLD DOMINATION. IT IS ABOUT SELF RECOGNITION, SELF UNDERSTANDING".

He noted that as Rastafari we are sighting [understanding] the things through nature. Rastafari has a lot more things in common with spiritual beliefs that come from cultures that existed long before Christianity".

When Mutaburaka said this I once again reflected on the connection and attraction that some Jamaicans especially Rastafarian have with indigenous peoples. Jamaica being the birthplace of Rastafari, a movement that formed countering an imposed colonial European mindset. As Mutaburaka stated "the intention of Rastafari is not to associate christian and biblical thought but is a way of life that has as its intention to liberate the minds and the physical being of black people from a system that one Rastafari founder Leonard Howell called a wicked system".

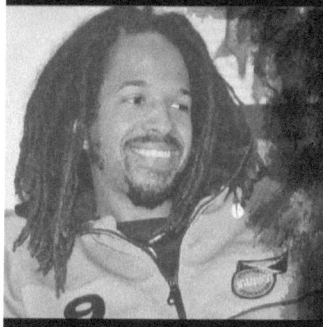

I remembered the friendship formed between a revolutionary Jamaican writer Dutty Bookman and an eight year Aboriginal child Apachita in Canada. Dutty in his book "Tried & True: Revelations Of A Rebellious Youth" details among other things his own spiritual journey and the immense positive effect Rastafari had on his personal evolvement. Apachita is a child who on different occasions I have turned to for advice because of her spiritual awareness, liberated mind and what I feel is her uncanny ability to see the things.

Apachita's mother wrote me and said when Apachita and Dutty met it was like they had known each other for years. It was like something was pulling them together. One day soon after encountering Dutty Bookman at a reggae concert I had the chance to speak to Apachita. I said ' do you remember Dutty the writer from Jamaica? He remembers you. He said he really liked talking to you".

Very excited and in such a sweet way Apachita said

"OH YES I REMEMBER HIM HE IS SUCH AN EXCELLENT MAN!"

Certainly in my life experience I have found children to be remarkably perceptive especially, if as in the case of Apachita, they are raised in a way that respects and affirms their own particular spiritual vision. The words of physcotherapist Bob Mannings came to mind. I remembered him speaking to me about black people who were searching for spirituality outside of the framework of the traditional church and how they were drawn to native spirituality.

It seemed to me the meeting of Apachita and Dutty symbolises the encounter of people from two different cultures brought together by their spiritual awareness . A coming together of black and aboriginal cultures in a manner that has the potential to offer so much to humanity.

Rebellious

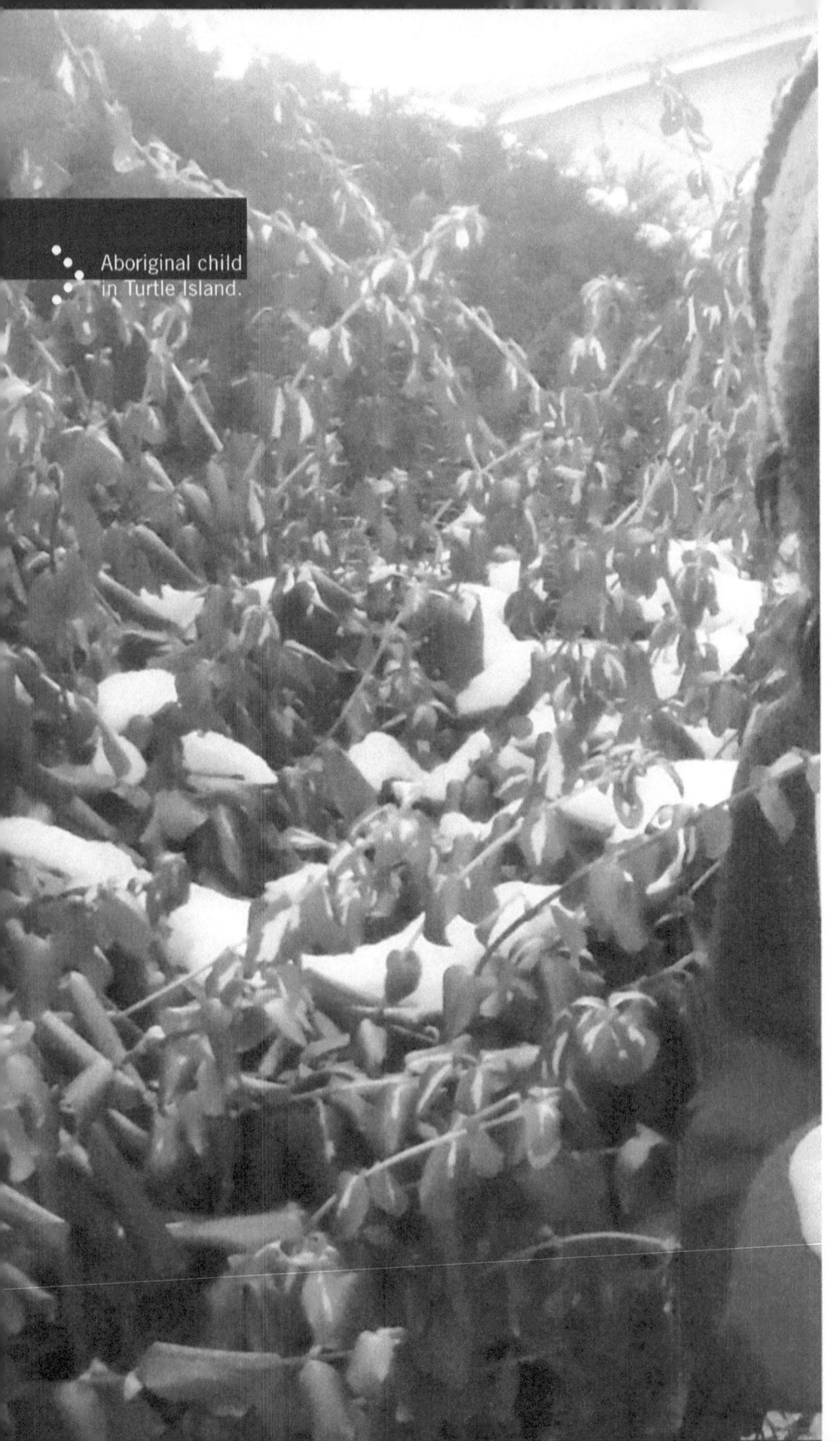

Aboriginal child in Turtle Island.

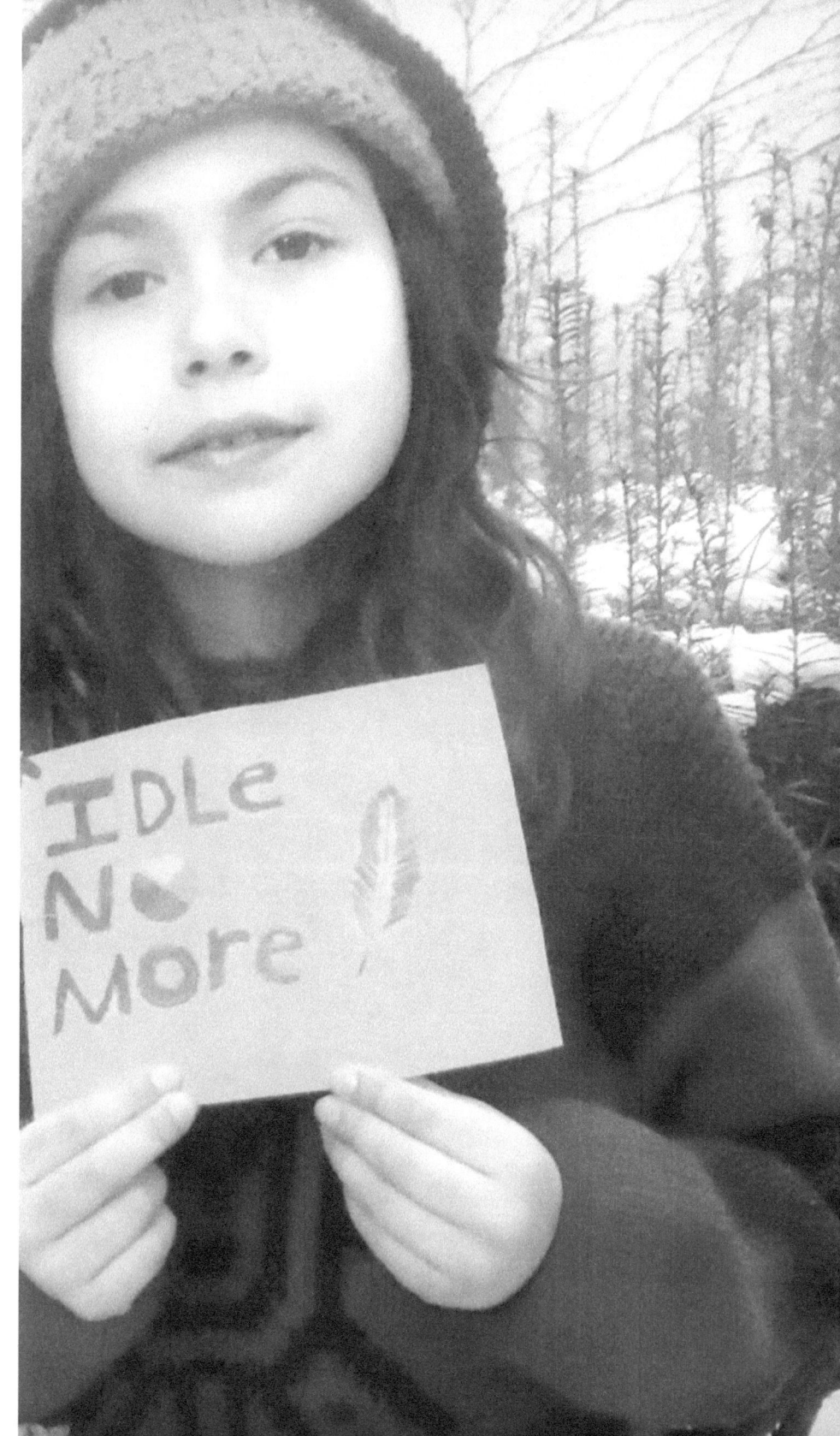

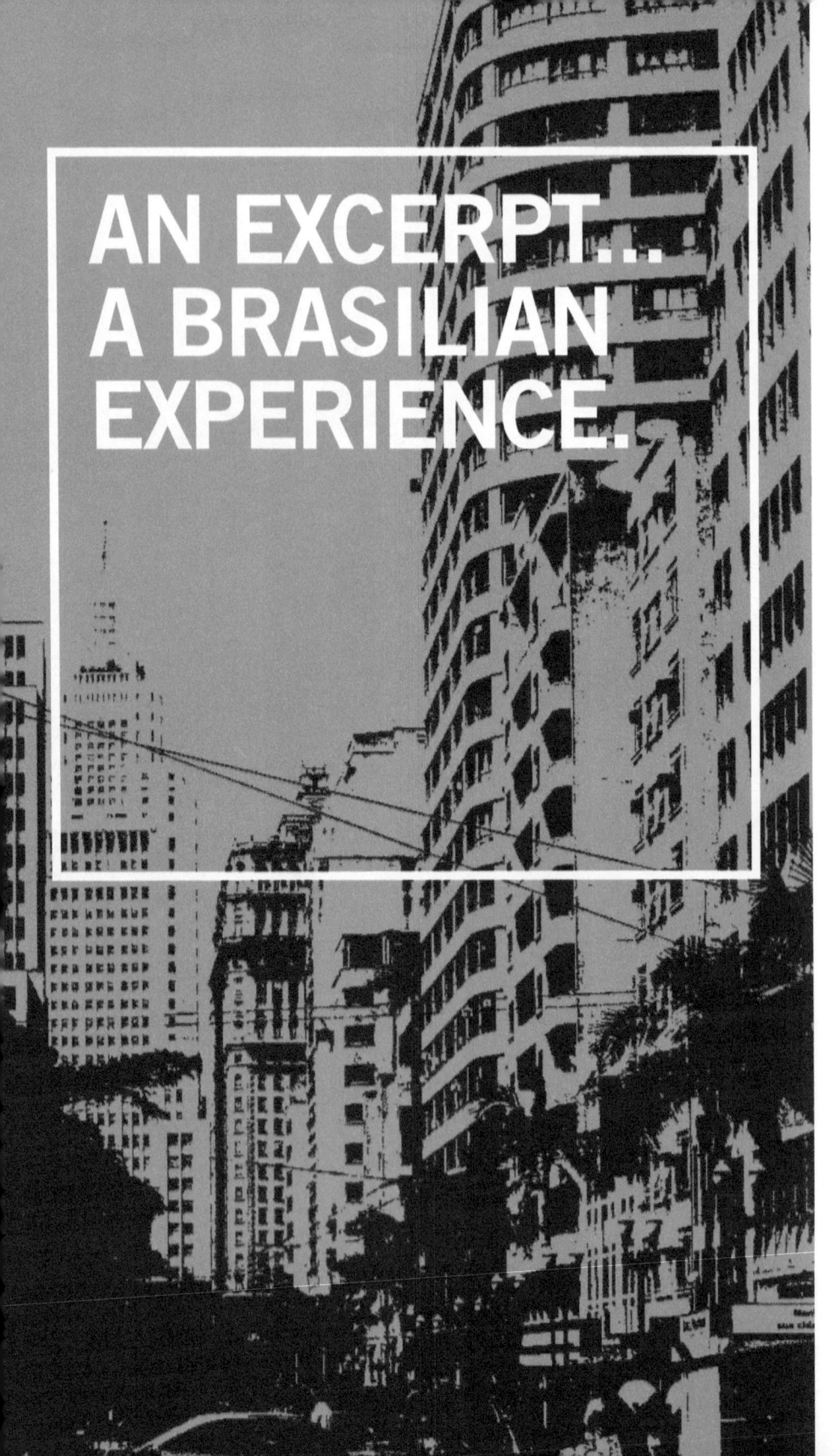

One day while walking the streets of Salvador, I saw a black woman who was selling a variety of religious objects. I immediately noticed that one of the objects for sale was a statue of an aboriginal man wearing a headdress. The vendor explained that the statues were used for purposes of protection by followers of the Afro Brasilian religion Umbanda. Having seen similar statues in the households of Santeria in Santiago, Cuba I knew right away that this pointed to a Blakk Indian spiritual link.

Some time later in the city of Sao Paulo I was attending a performance by an Afro Brasilian dance company. Unlike, similar companies, they included an interpretation of Umbanda. As part of the theatrical presentation they had an authority on Umbanda planted in the audience who answered questions posed by the cast members about the religion. After the performance, I asked him some questions about the significance of Aboriginal spirits in Umbanda. He introduced himself as Pai Sydney de Xango, a high priest of Umbanda. We had a great conversation and he paid great attention to the links I was able to point out to him between Aboriginal people and voodoo in Haiti. As a result of our conversation he invited me to an Umbanda ceremony that would be held at his family's house.

The next week I arrived at his house at midnight. From outside the house I could hear the sound of African drumming and singing. I was ushered into a large room where the Umbanda ceremony was occurring. I was greeted by Pai Sydney de Xango who was directing a group of white clad participants as they danced and chanted around large ceremonial objects in the room to the sound of African rhythms provided by a group of percussionists. As I looked around I noticed that in one corner room was a statue of a Black woman wearing the traditional white Umbanda clothing. In the other corner was a statue of an Aboriginal man wearing a headdress.

Hanging from the ceiling was a pot filled with feathers and feathers were also attached to an object hanging from one of the walls. I knew enough about the religious symbolism to understand that these feathers were representing a spiritual connection with the spirits of the Aboriginal ancestors of Brasil. Pai Sydney conducted the ceremony in the West African language of Yoruba. At various points in the ceremony different spirits possessed the participants. Their entire demeanor was transformed as they danced possessed under the careful guidance of Pai Sydney and his assistants who took them through various rituals. Homage was paid to various African gods (Orixas) and participants would come out dressed in various incredible costumes and masks to represent specific Orixas.

THROUGHOUT THE CEREMONY THE ENERGY IN THE ROOM WAS ELECTRIC.

There was non-stop drumming and chanting and the graceful movements of Pai Sydney as he danced while chanting prayers and incantations in Yoruba. At one point in the ceremony a young boy who was about nine years old, wearing only white pants and with the rest of his body painted with white dots was given the spotlight of the ceremony as only he and Pai Sydney danced around the room. The young boy danced using traditional Yoruba moves singing incantations until he went into a state of trance. This was a major step for the young boy and all who were present gave him applause for his efforts.

When the ceremony finished at four that morning, pots of traditional Bahian and Nigerian cooking were brought out and all the participants and their guests and relatives were served by Pai Sydney and his assistants. Afterwards people hung out and socialized. While waiting to speak with Pai Sydney I spoke with one of the participants who turned out to be the aunt of the young boy who had been dancing in the ceremony. She informed me that this night marked the eighteenth anniversary of her coming to Umbanda. She also revealed to me that her father was aboriginal and her mother was African.

After the food was consumed, I had a chance to speak with Pai Sydney. He explained to me that in the late nineteenth century Allan Kardec brought a form of spiritualism to Brasil. Allan Kardec was a French writer who in the nineteenth century wrote several books on spiritualism and mediums. These books reached Brasil and groups were started which were based on this writing, giving rise to the movement known as Kardecismo. This spiritualism had its origin in Europe and was very Euro centric. At some point in the 1870s followers of Kardenismo were having a séance when an Aboriginal spirit tried to come into the session but the White practitioners wouldn't let it enter. The aboriginal spirit said that a new religion should be formed that would respect and incorporate the spirits of Black and aboriginal ancestors. The first Umbanda house was established in Recife during the 1870s and was called "tenda de umbanda do caboclo das sete encruzilhadas "

> One of the tenets which distinguish Umbanda with other Afro Brasilian religions such as Candomble is the space and respect that it gives to the aboriginal spirits known as Cabocle.

[I should point out that I was told that possibly a very early form of Candomble' called Candomble d' Angola might have had Aboriginal spiritual links but this is a very difficult area to research.]

There are various Aboriginal spirits in Umbanda such as Iron Chest, White Feathers, and Seven Arrows. As Pai Sydney told me, often on the altars at Umbanda temples you will see Aboriginal statues and feathers that signify those spirits. I didn't witness this at this particular ceremony, but I have been informed that there are

Umbanda ceremonies that invoke the aboriginal spirits who speak through the devotees and suggest potions and incantations for those with medical problems. He also explained to me that Umbanda wanted to respect and honor the spirits of the ancestors of the Aboriginal people of Brasil, on whose land they were.

This was the reason that there was a statue of the aboriginal man in the corner of the room as one enters. While it was clear to me that the focus of Umbanda was on its traditional African roots, its practitioners went out of their way to honor the aboriginal presence and spirits in their ceremonies. One Aboriginal observer who was present at the ceremony commented to me that if Europeans had shown this type of respect for aboriginal culture when they arrived in Brasil, perhaps the devastation of "aboriginal people in Brasil wouldn't have occurred.

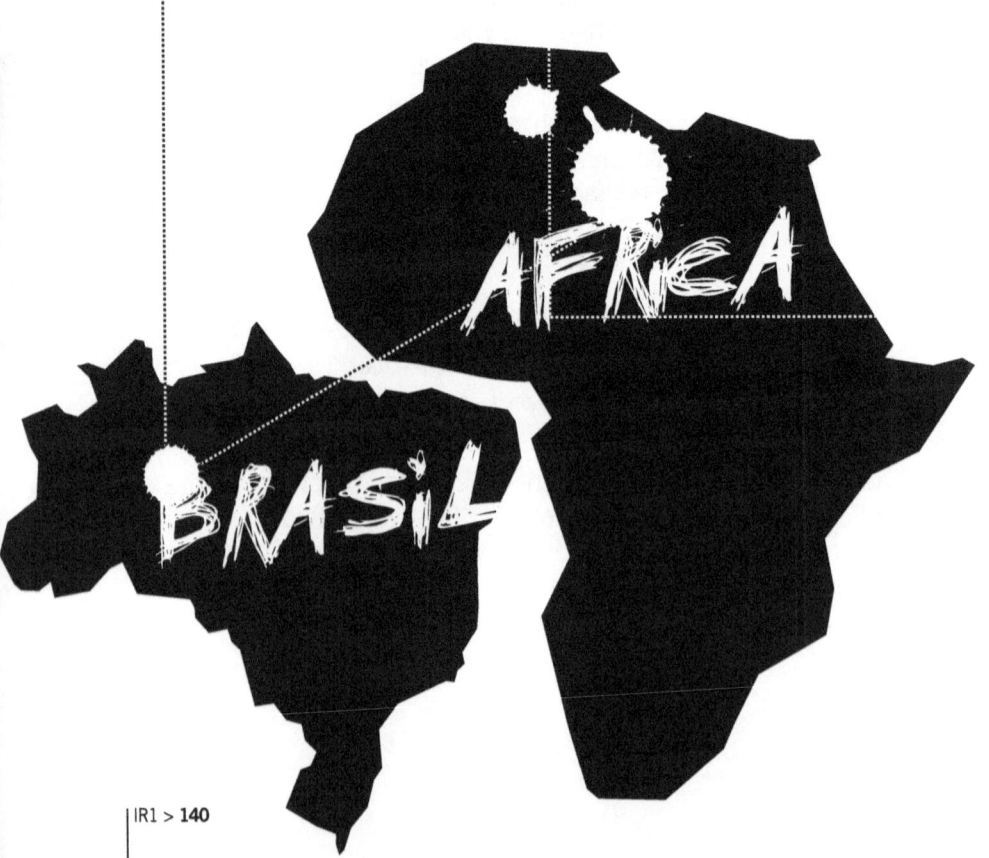

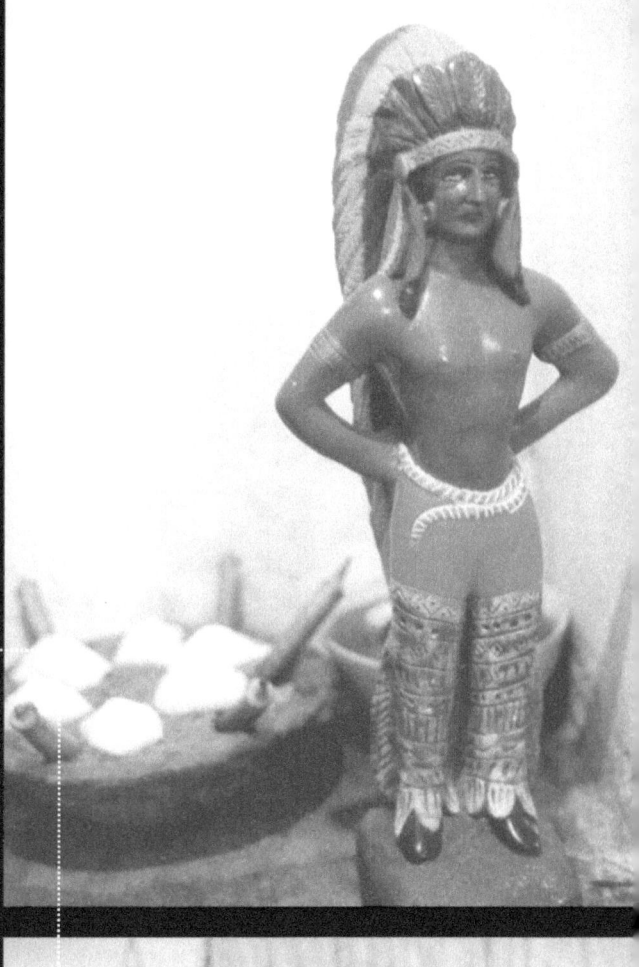

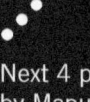
Next 4 photos by Mapuchedub. Umbanda ceremony in São Paulo, Brasil.

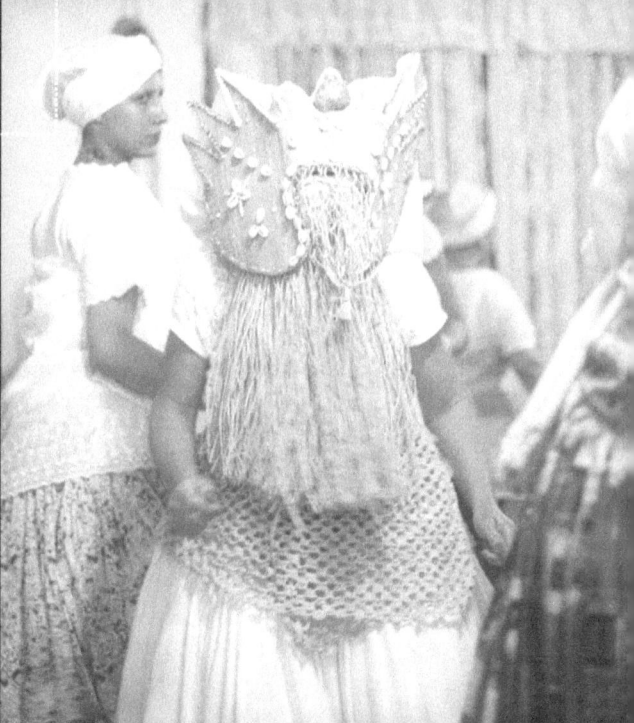

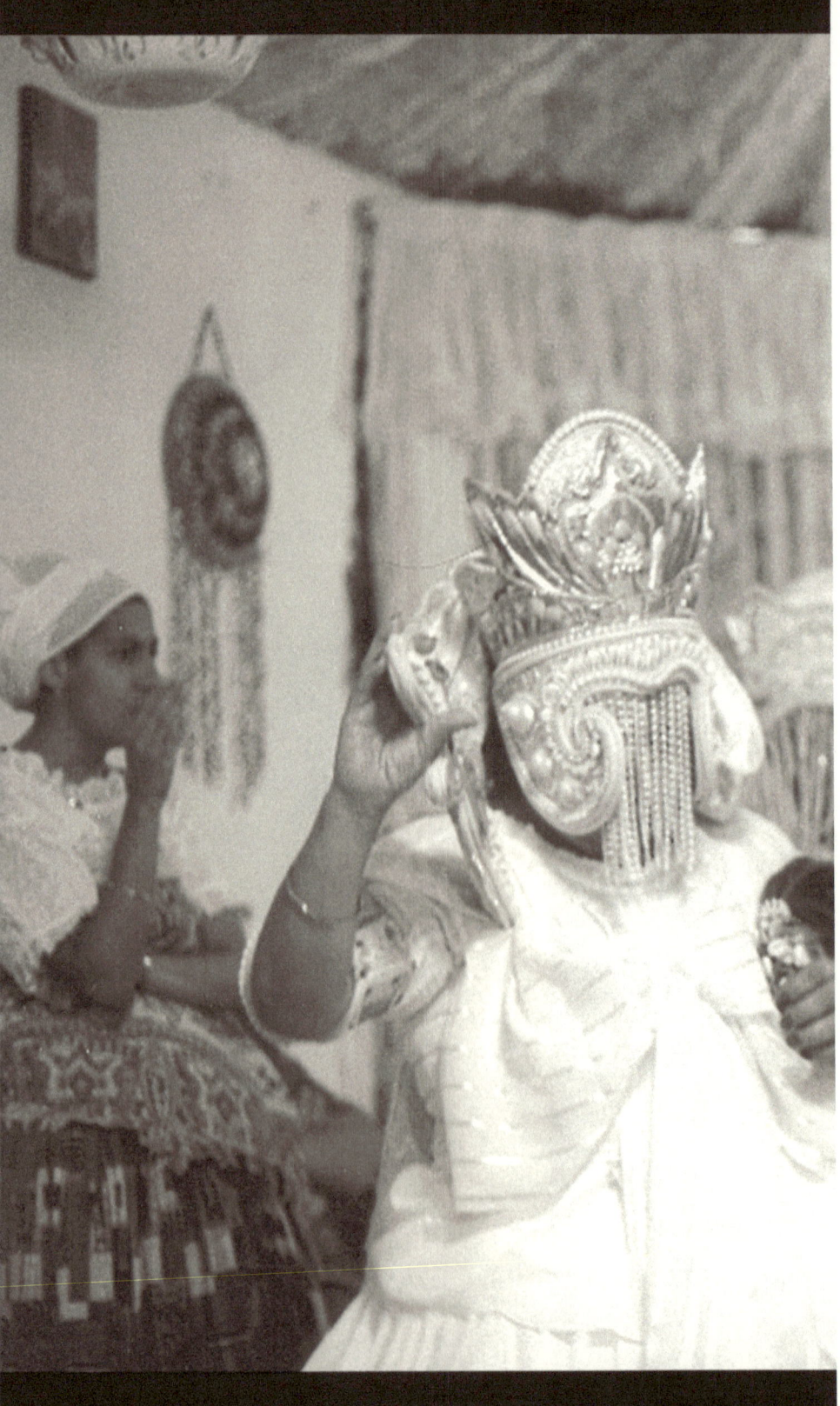

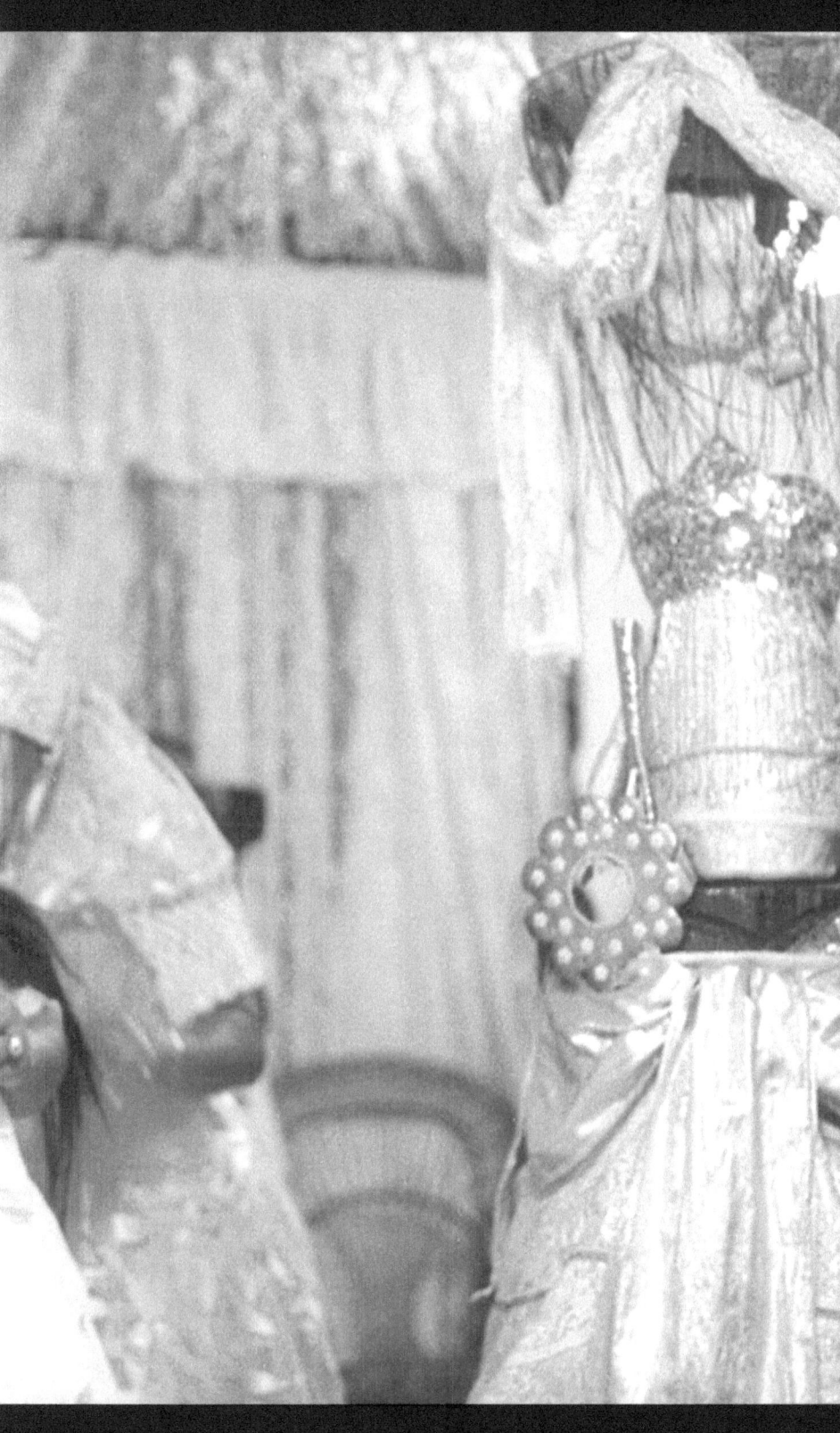

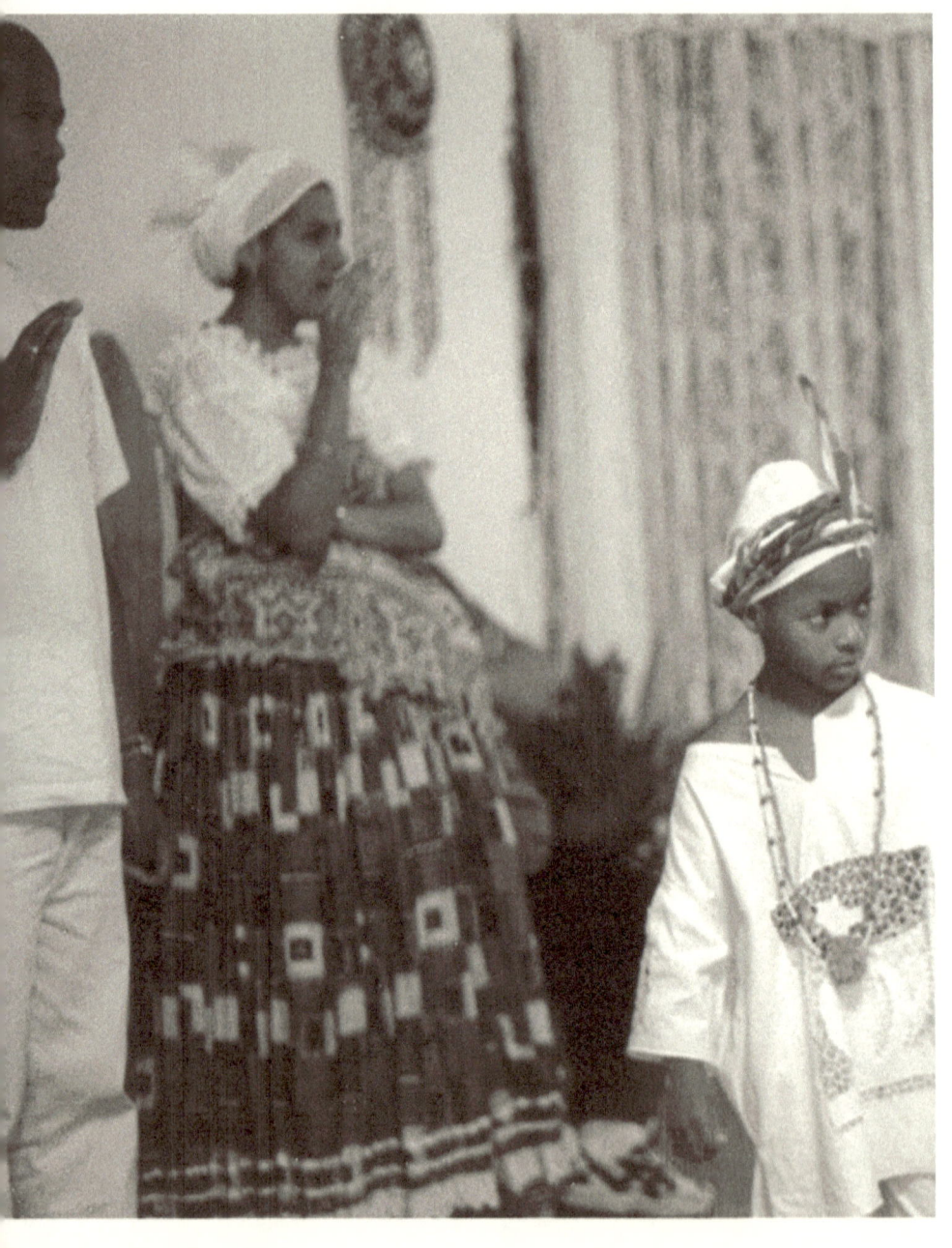

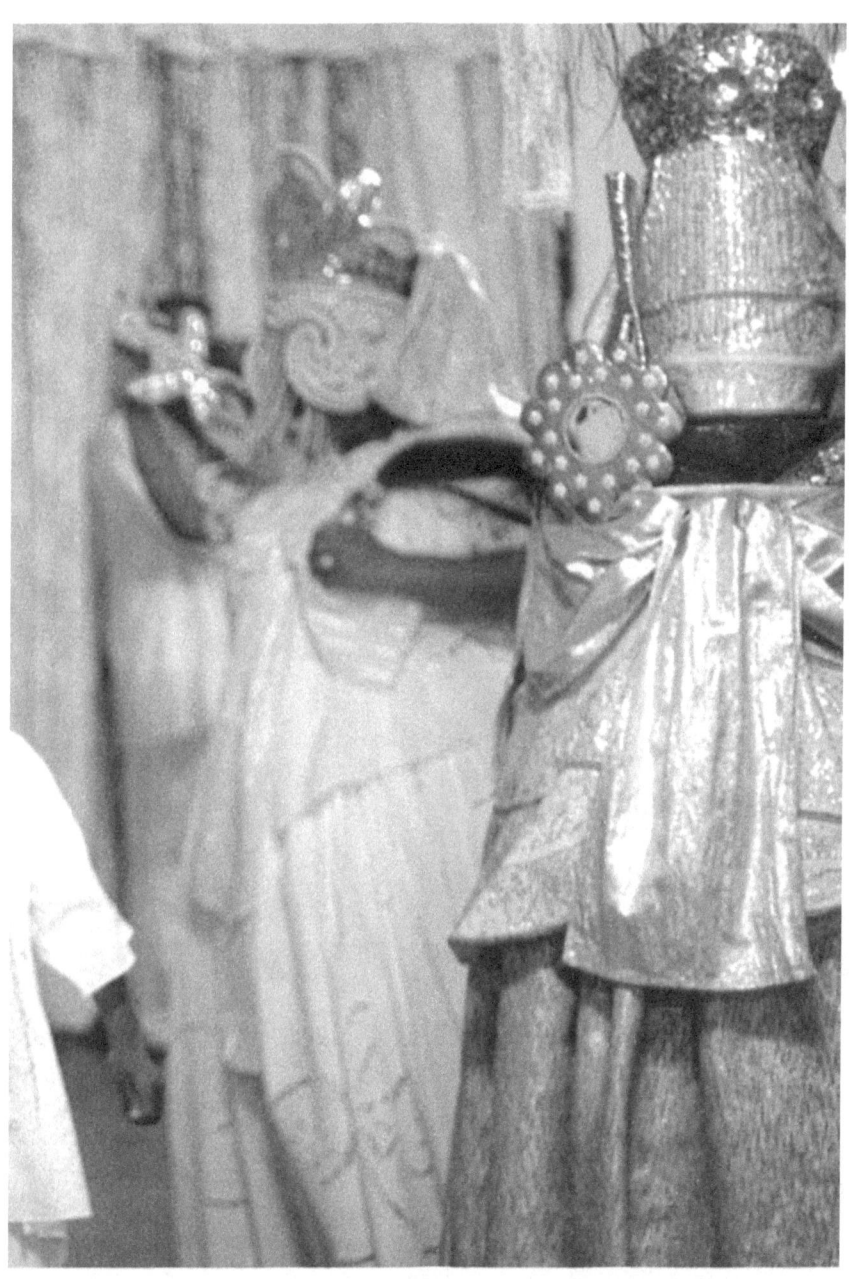

THE VISUAL REVOLUTION

MIX 2

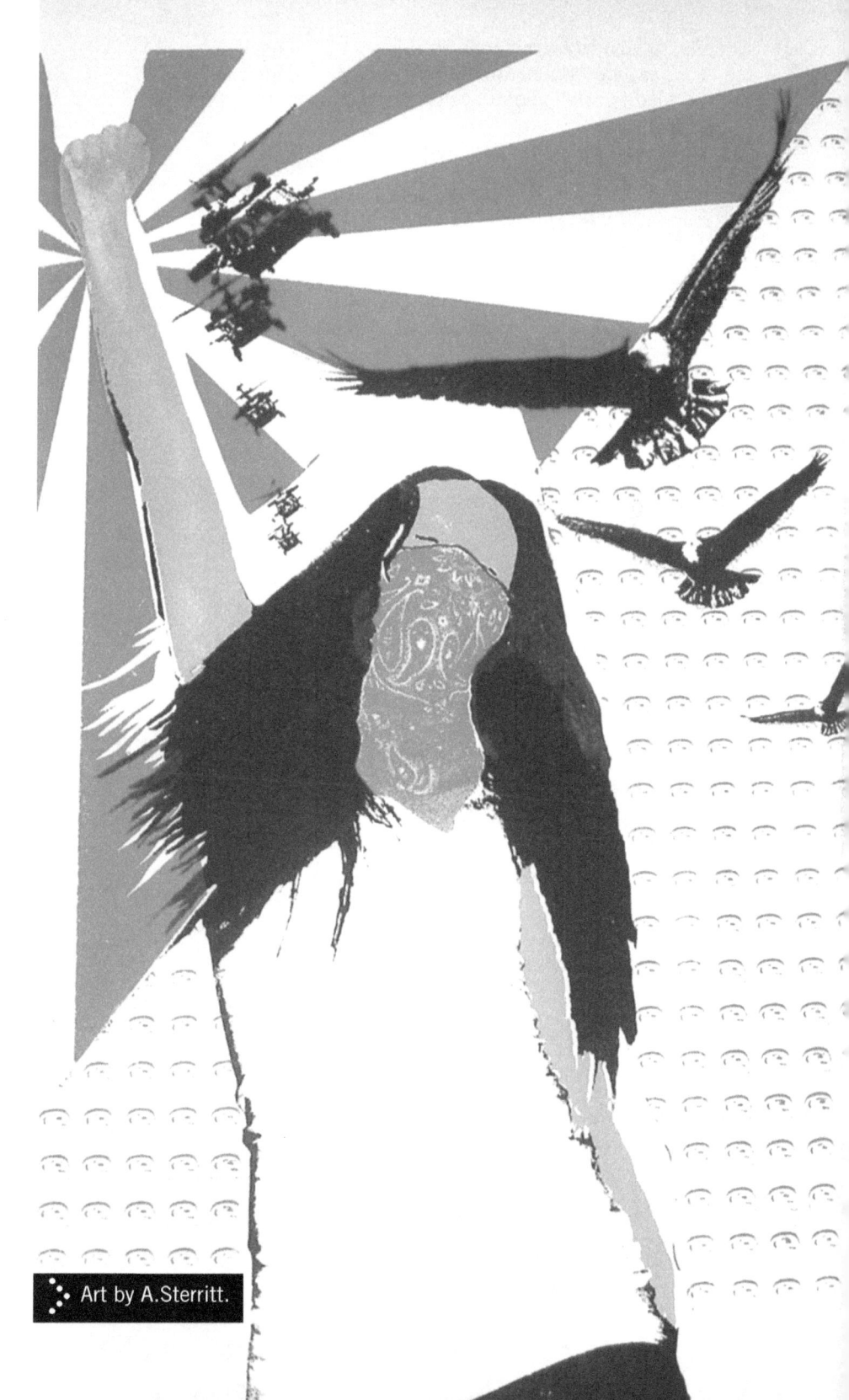
Art by A.Sterritt.

IR/Chite Yarumo mural in Candelaria, Bogota, Colombia.
Mural shows Jah 9, Haunani-Kay Trask & Chief Poundmaker.
You can read translation of whats on mural in page 33 of IR30.

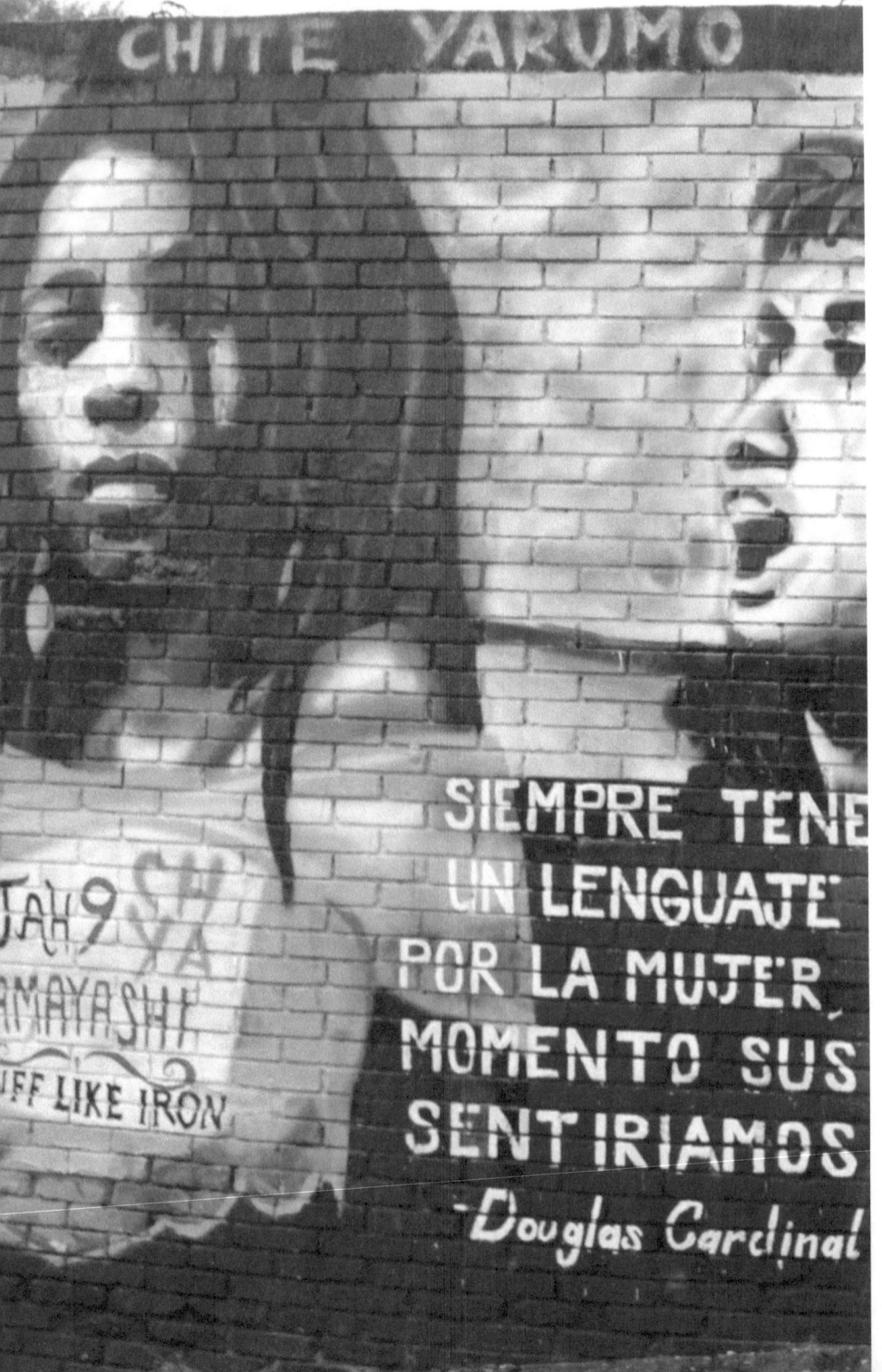

...MOS QUE RECREAR
... QUE MUESTRE RESPETO
... SI CAMINARAMOS UN
... ZAPATOS NOS
... INDIGNADOS.

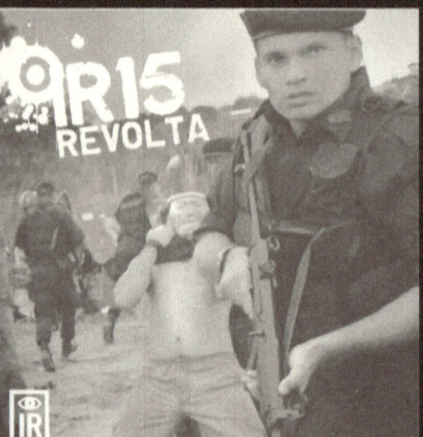
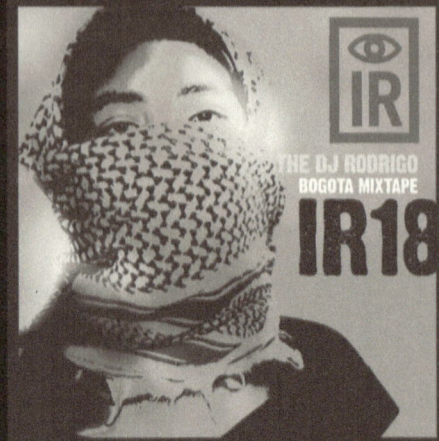
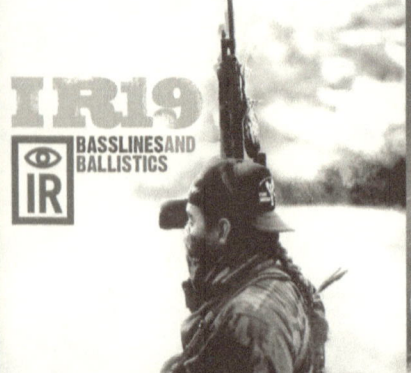
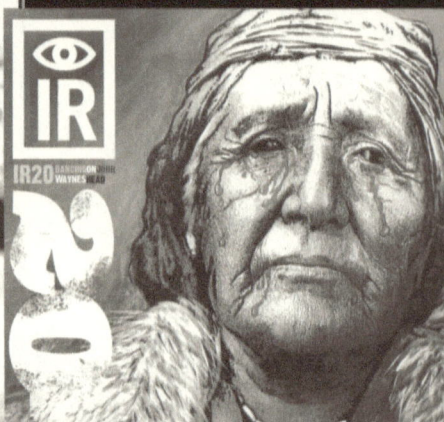
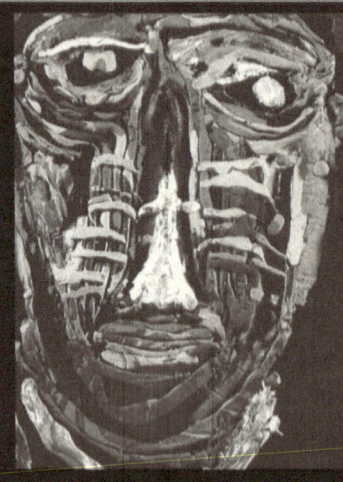
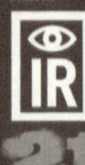
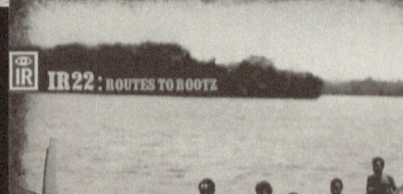
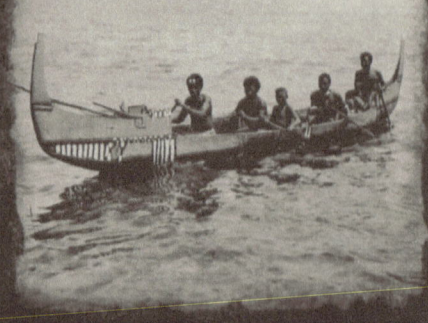

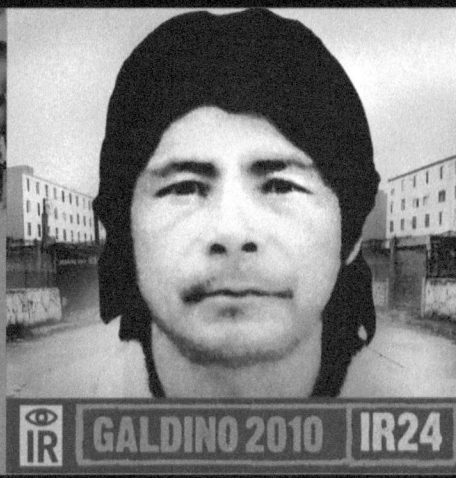
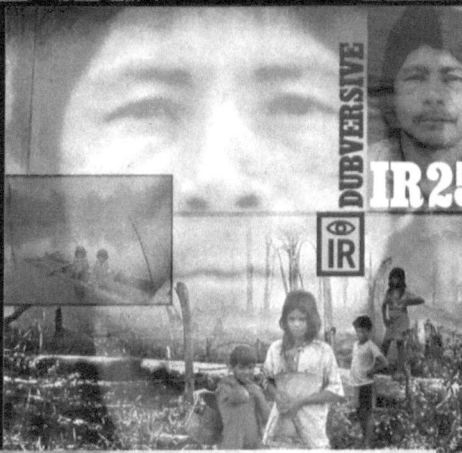
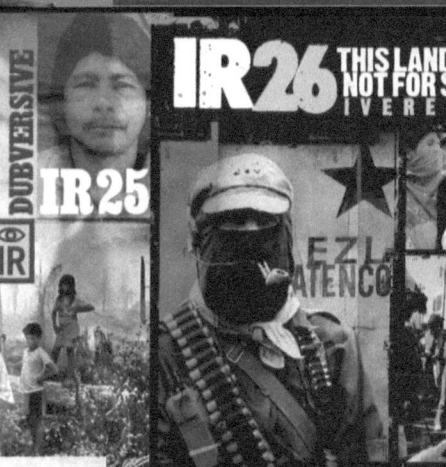
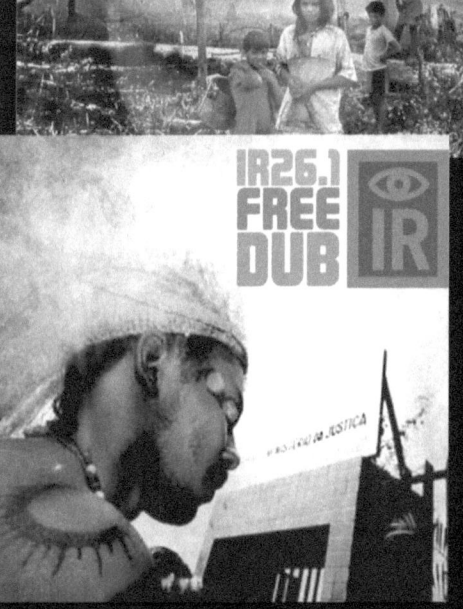
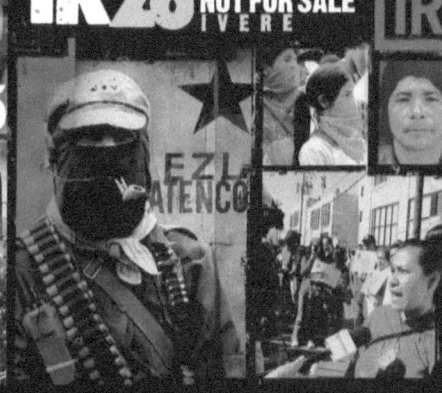
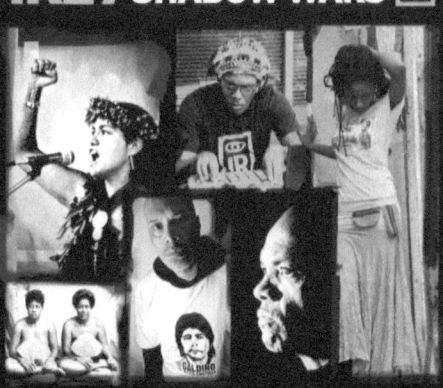

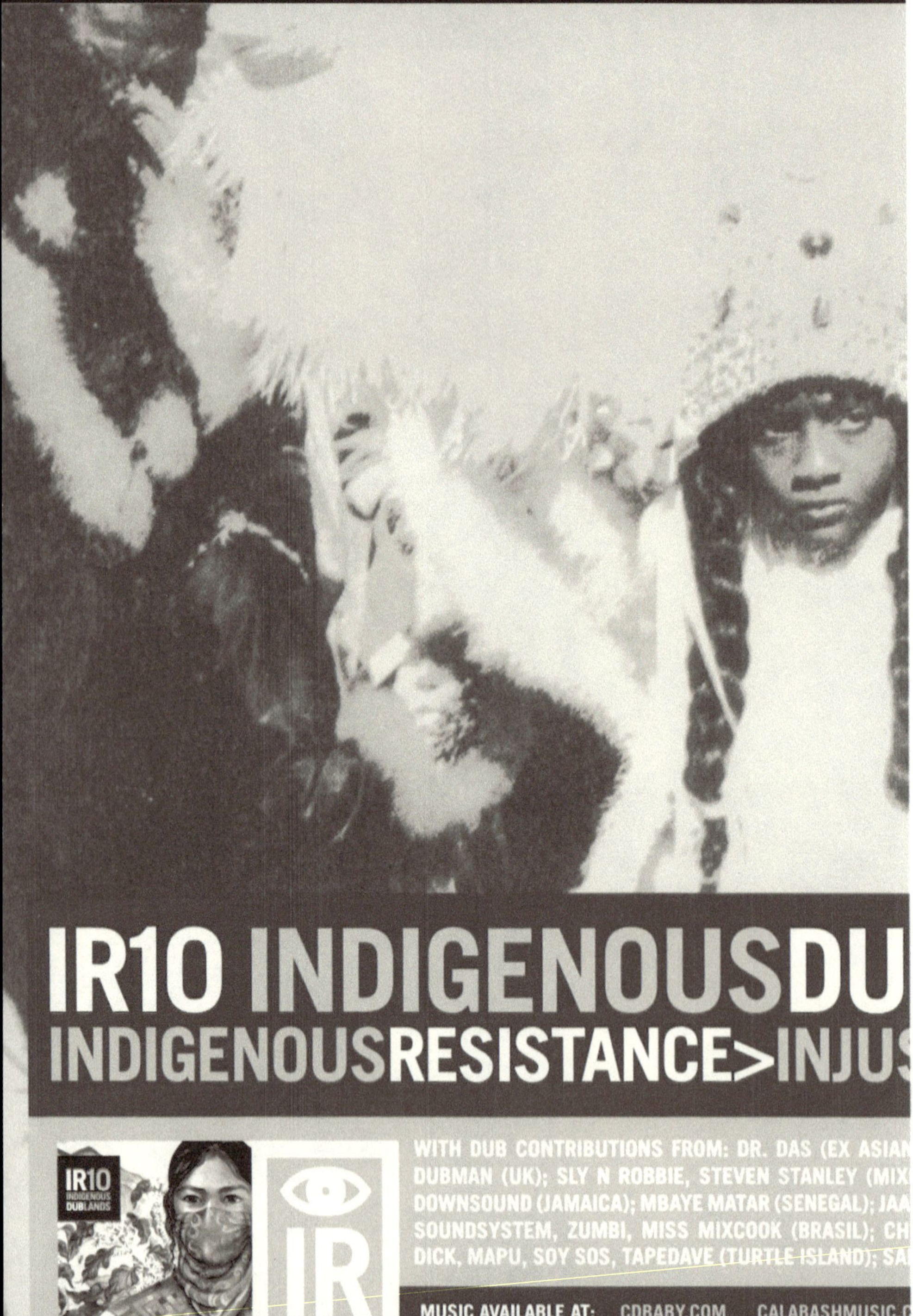

IR10 INDIGENOUSDU
INDIGENOUSRESISTANCE>INJUS

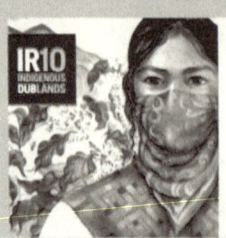
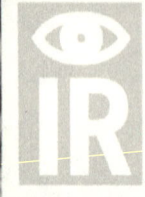

WITH DUB CONTRIBUTIONS FROM: DR. DAS (EX ASIAN
DUBMAN (UK); SLY N ROBBIE, STEVEN STANLEY (MIX
DOWNSOUND (JAMAICA); MBAYE MATAR (SENEGAL); JAA
SOUNDSYSTEM, ZUMBI, MISS MIXCOOK (BRASIL); CH
DICK, MAPU, SOY SOS, TAPEDAVE (TURTLE ISLAND); SA

MUSIC AVAILABLE AT: __CDBABY.COM __CALABASHMUSIC.C

BLANDS
STICEREZIST

DUB FOUNDATION), RAMJAC, BOBBY
MASTER FOR TOM TOM CLUB,B 52s),
BI (SOUTH PACIFIC ISLANDS); DUBDEM
RISTIANE D, JAMIE CANFIELD, JIMMY
EVO, TOHUNUNO (SOLOMON ISLANDS).

OM__ ITUNES __WWW.DUBREALITY.COM

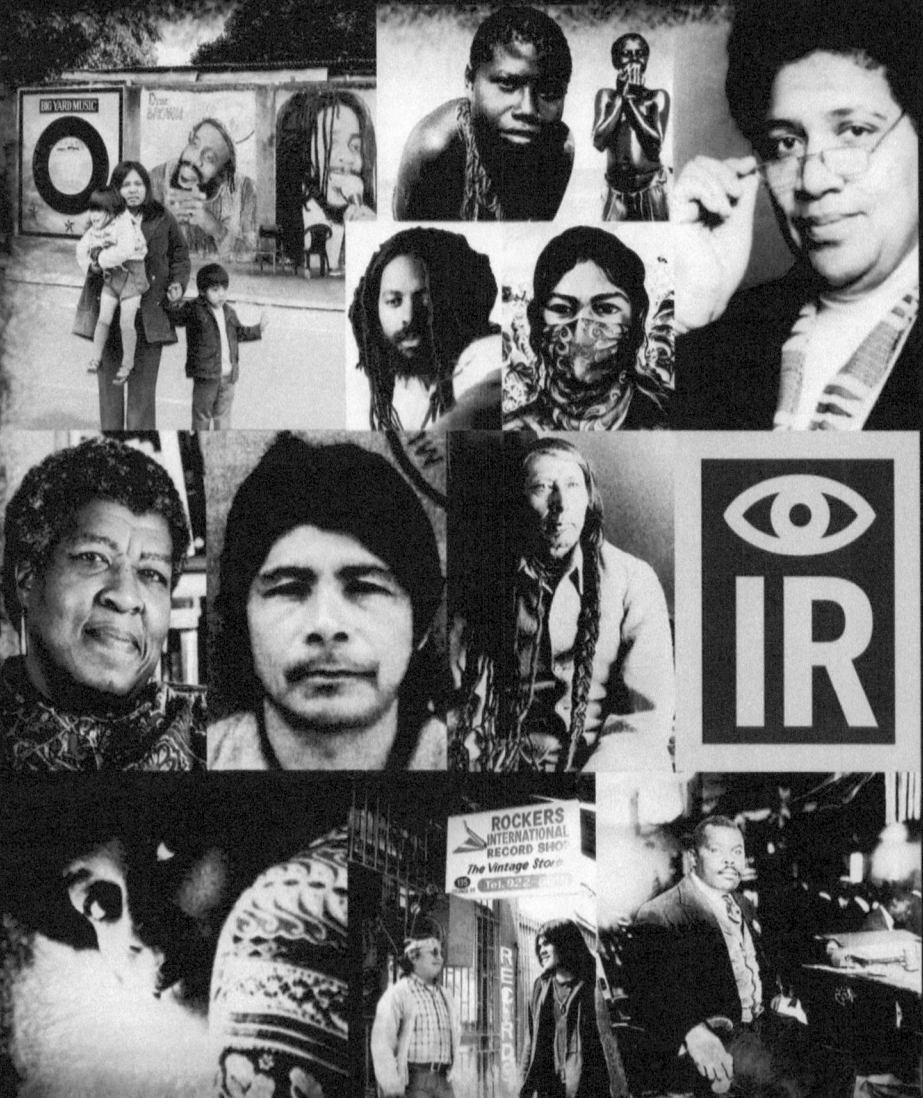

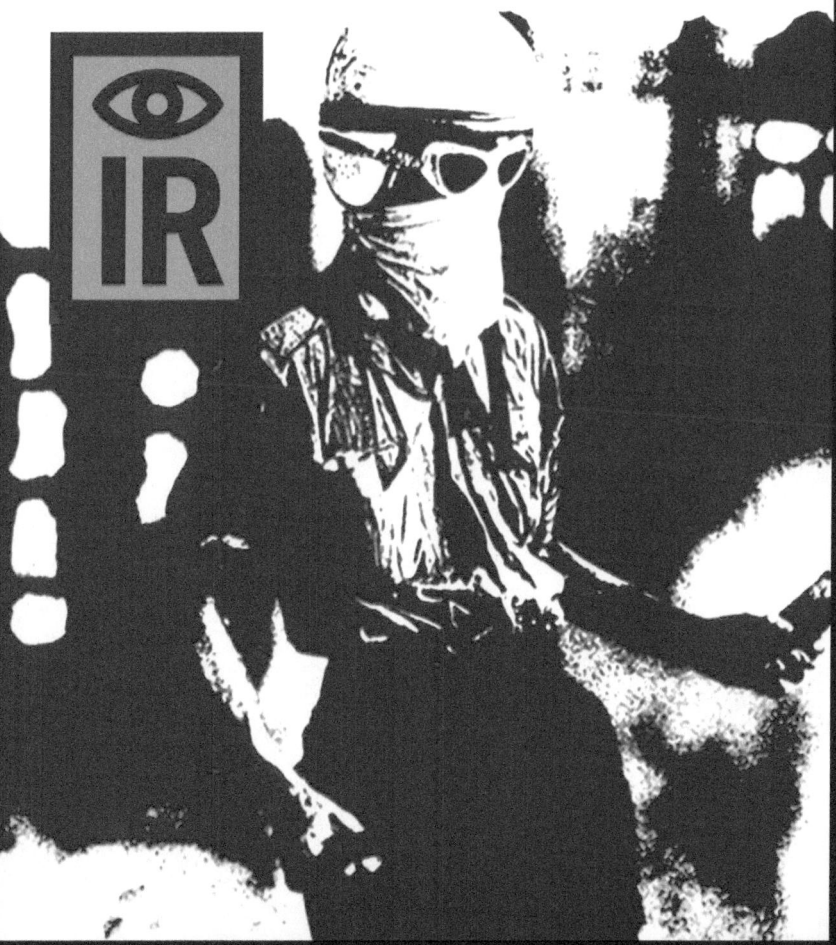

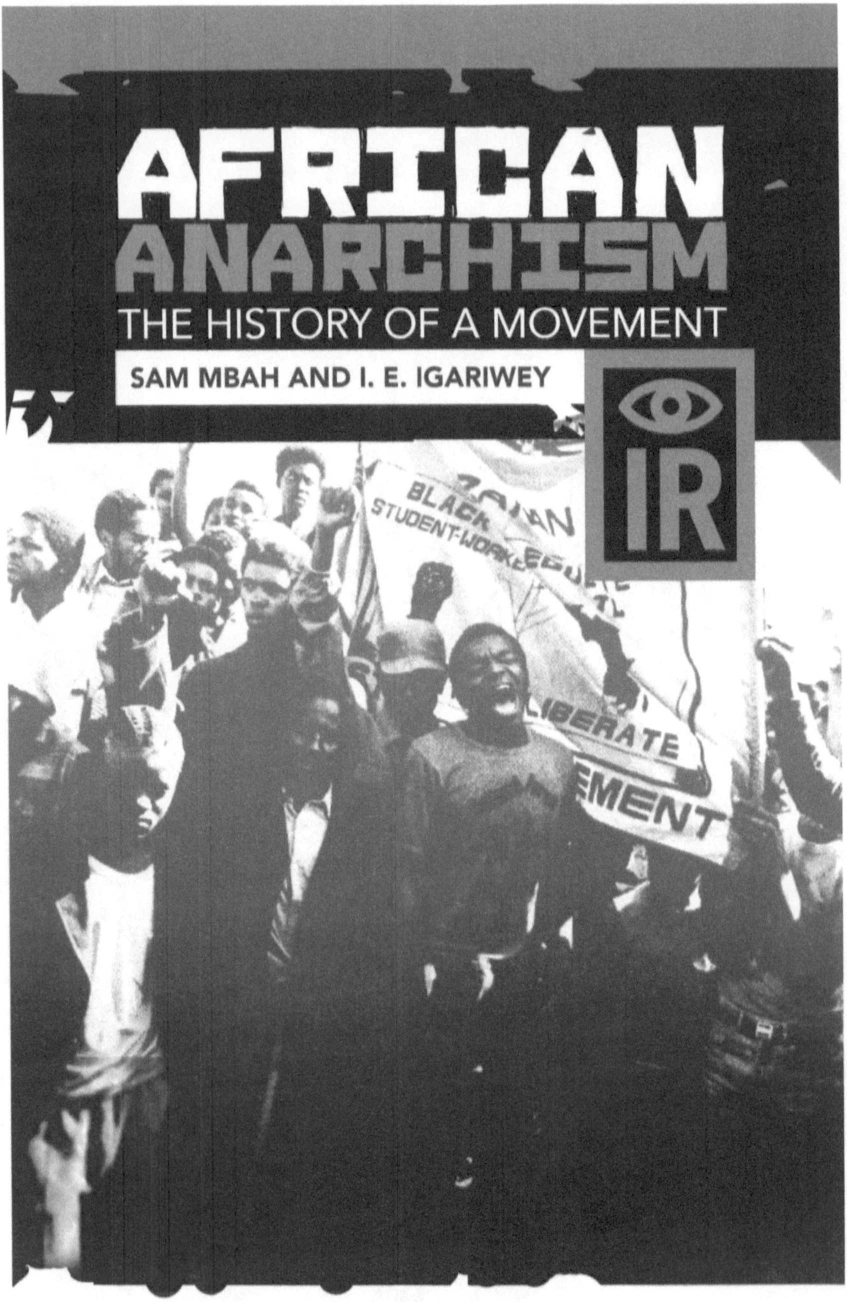

AFRICAN ANARCHISM
THE HISTORY OF A MOVEMENT
SAM MBAH AND I. E. IGARIWEY

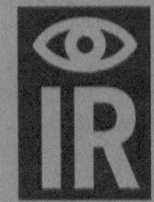

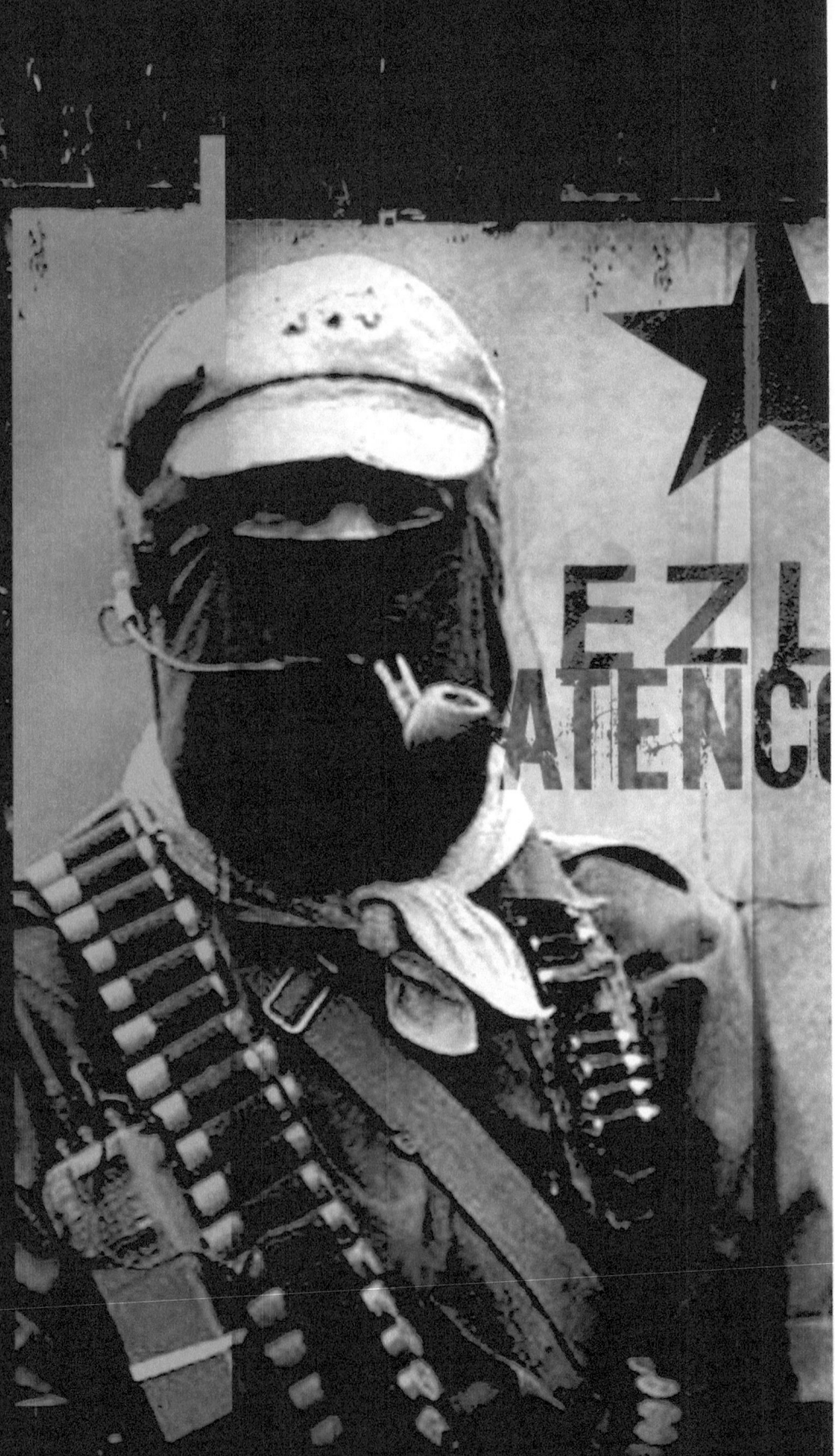

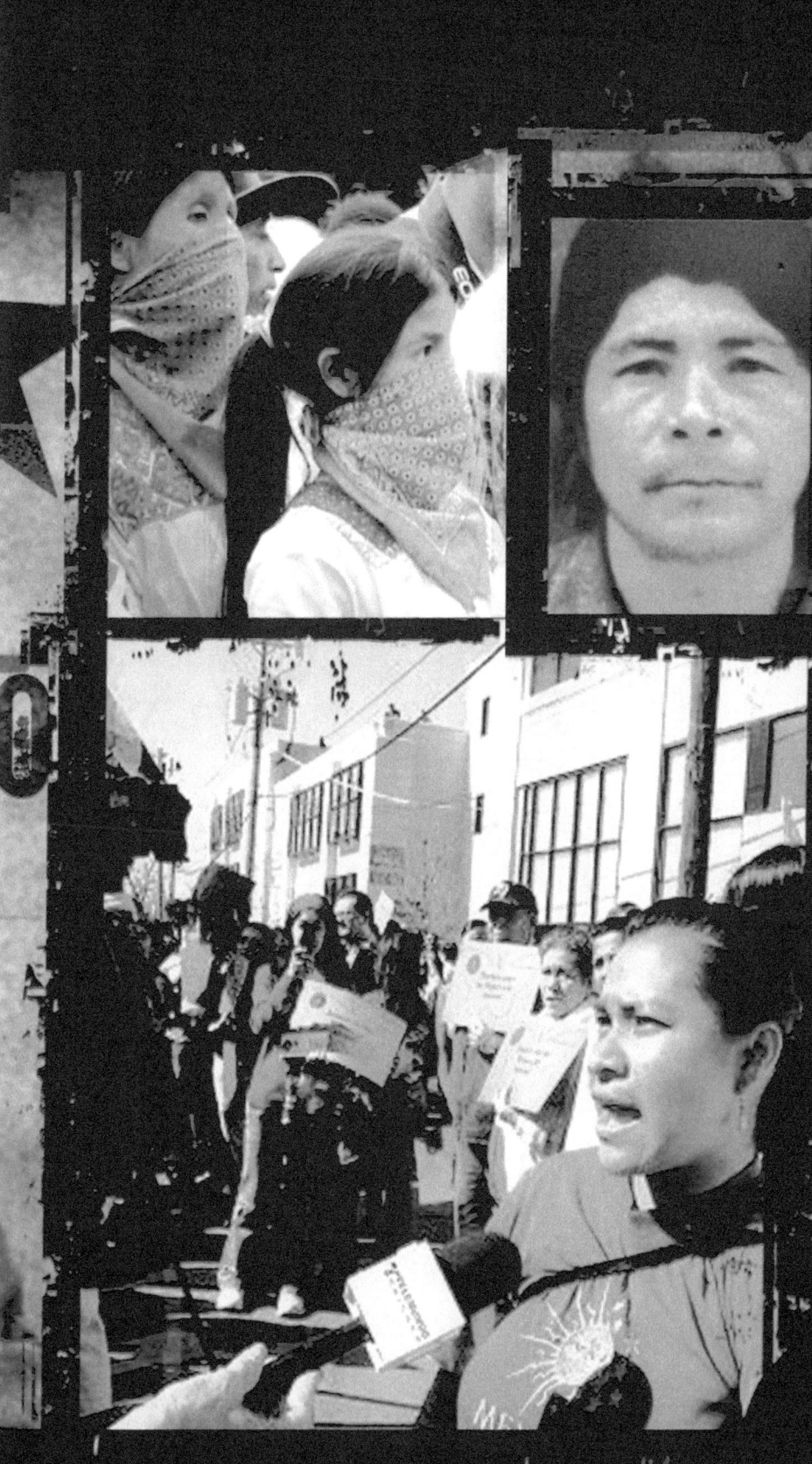

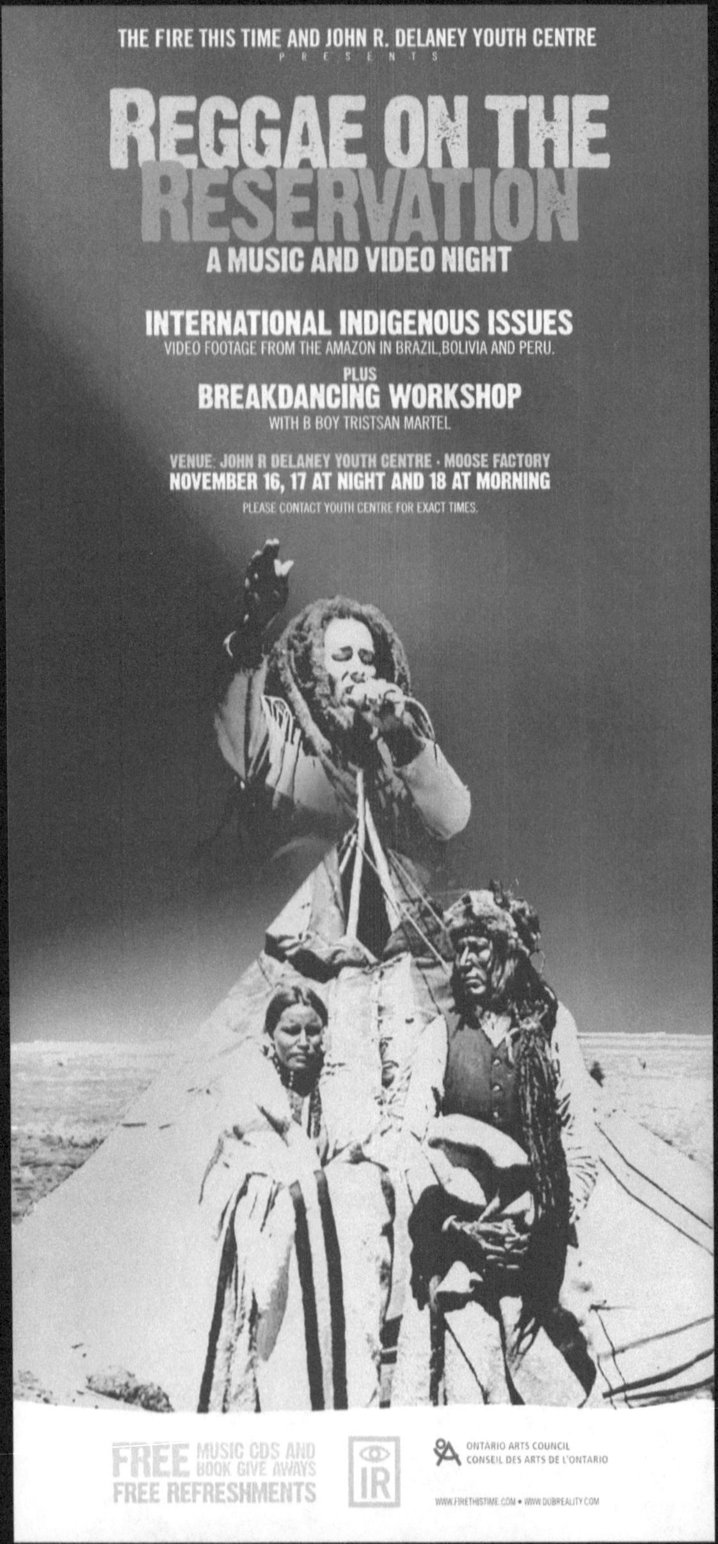

REGGAE ON THE RESERVATION
A MUSIC AND VIDEO NIGHT

THE FIRE THIS TIME AND JOHN R. DELANEY YOUTH CENTRE PRESENTS

INTERNATIONAL INDIGENOUS ISSUES
VIDEO FOOTAGE FROM THE AMAZON IN BRAZIL, BOLIVIA AND PERU.

PLUS

BREAKDANCING WORKSHOP
WITH B BOY TRISTSAN MARTEL

VENUE: JOHN R DELANEY YOUTH CENTRE · MOOSE FACTORY
NOVEMBER 16, 17 AT NIGHT AND 18 AT MORNING

PLEASE CONTACT YOUTH CENTRE FOR EXACT TIMES.

FREE MUSIC CDS AND BOOK GIVE AWAYS
FREE REFRESHMENTS

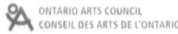

ONTARIO ARTS COUNCIL
CONSEIL DES ARTS DE L'ONTARIO

WWW.FIRETHISTIME.COM • WWW.DUBREALITY.COM

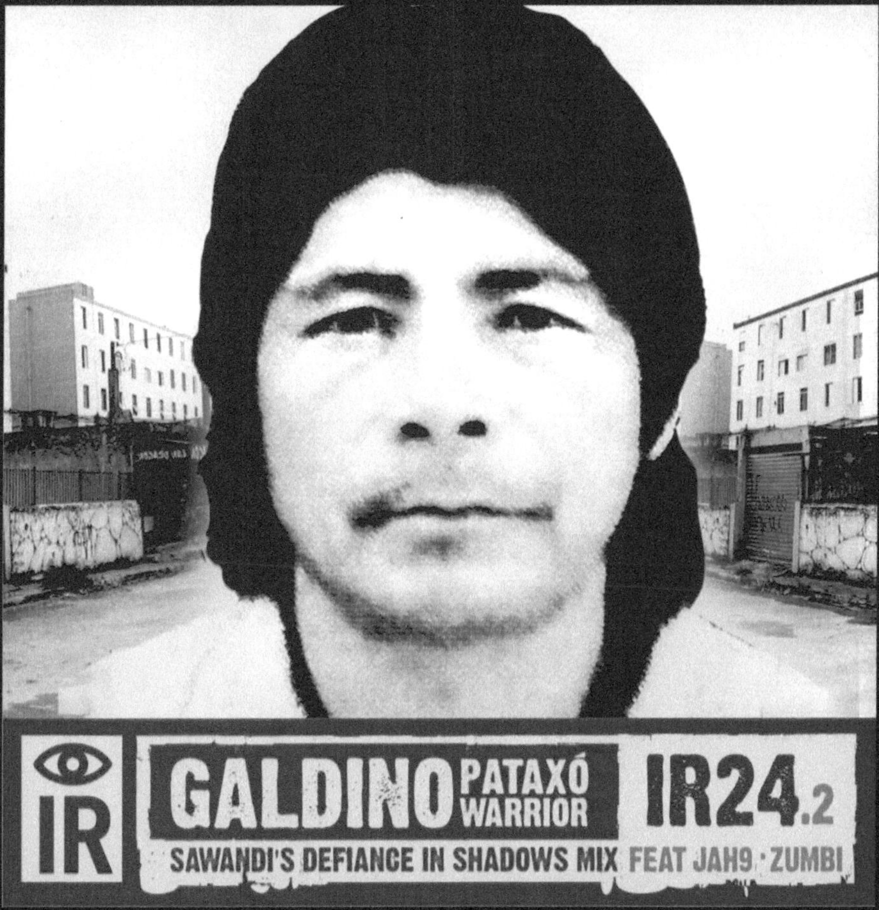

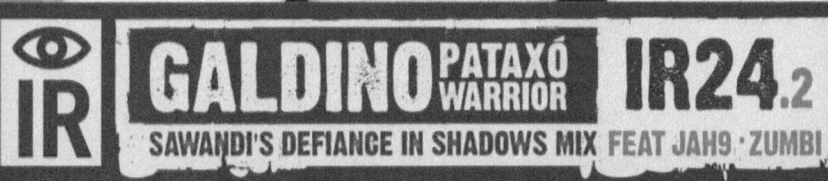

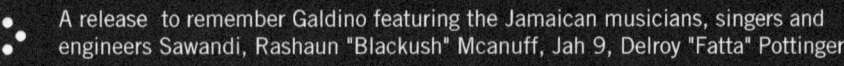

A release to remember Galdino featuring the Jamaican musicians, singers and engineers Sawandi, Rashaun "Blackush" Mcanuff, Jah 9, Delroy "Fatta" Pottinger".

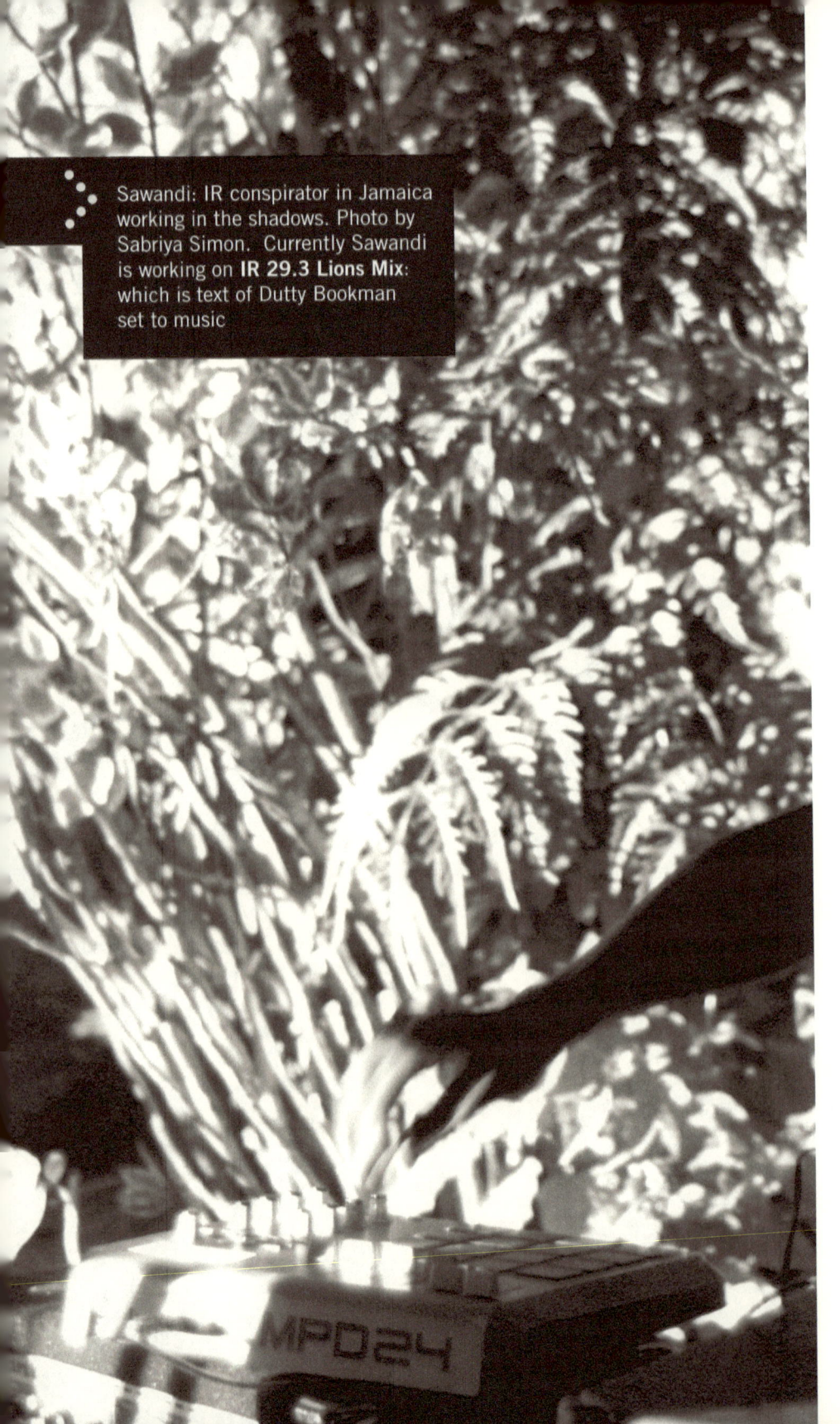

Sawandi: IR conspirator in Jamaica working in the shadows. Photo by Sabriya Simon. Currently Sawandi is working on **IR 29.3 Lions Mix**: which is text of Dutty Bookman set to music

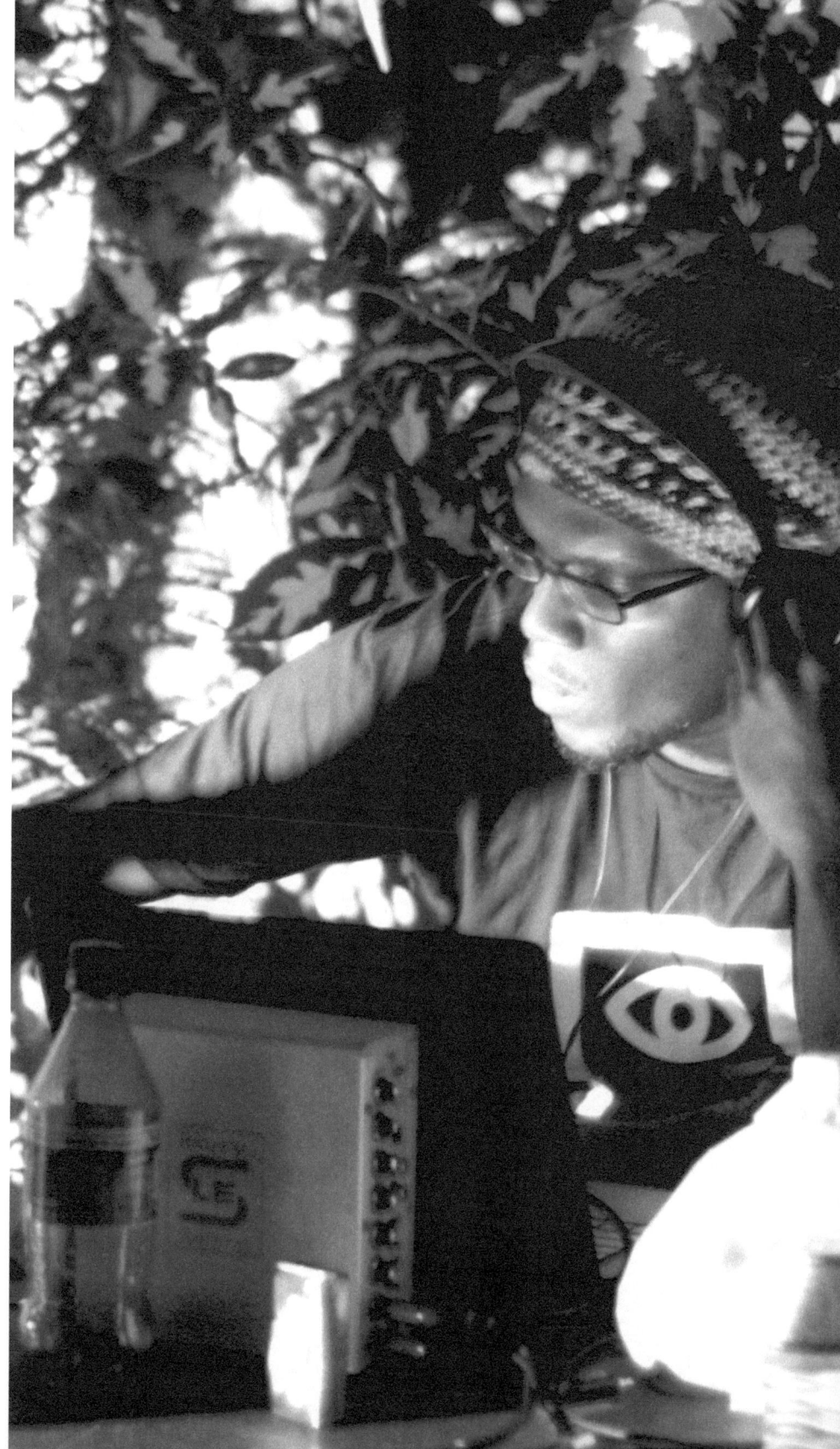

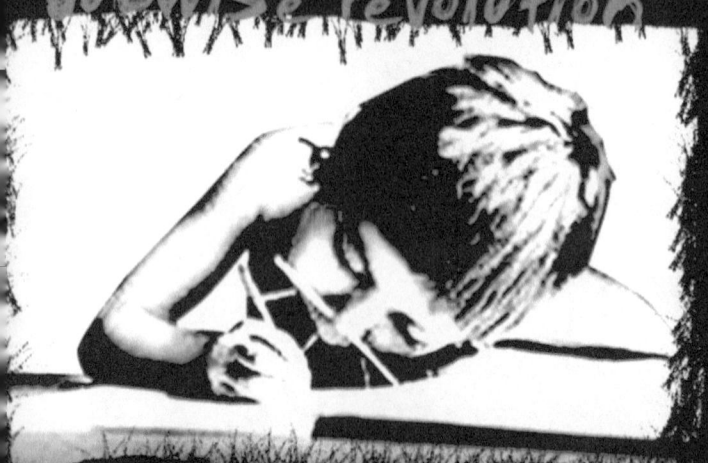

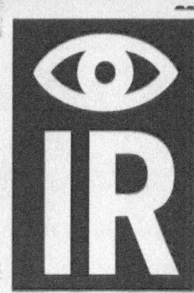
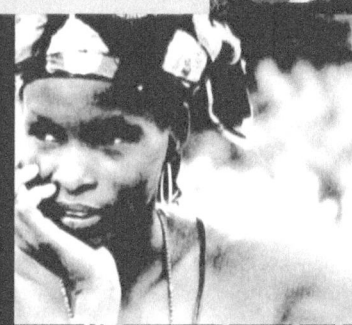
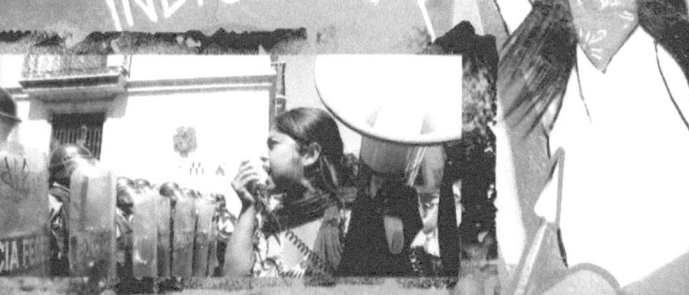

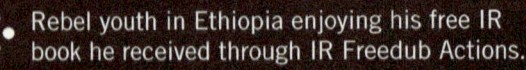

Rebel youth in Ethiopia enjoying his free IR book he received through IR Freedub Actions.

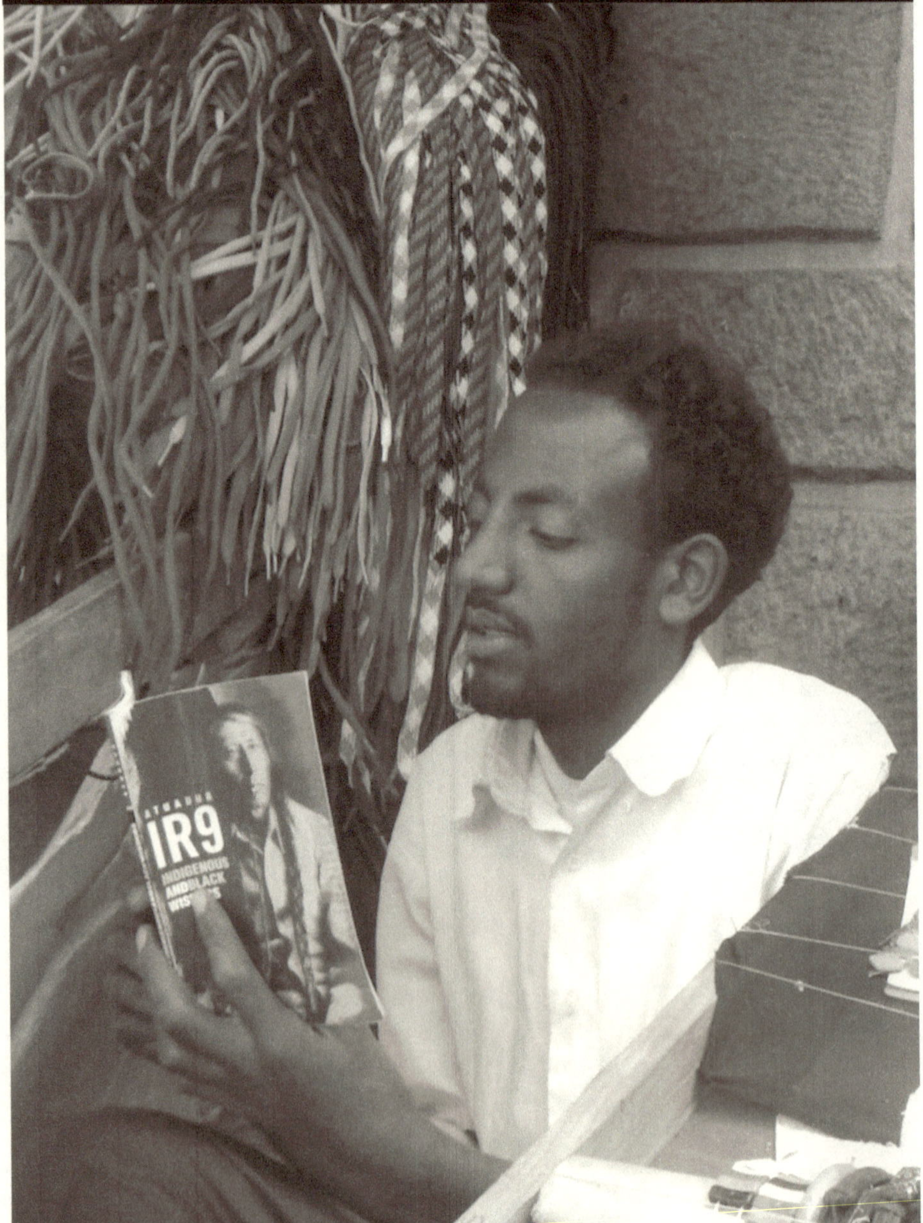

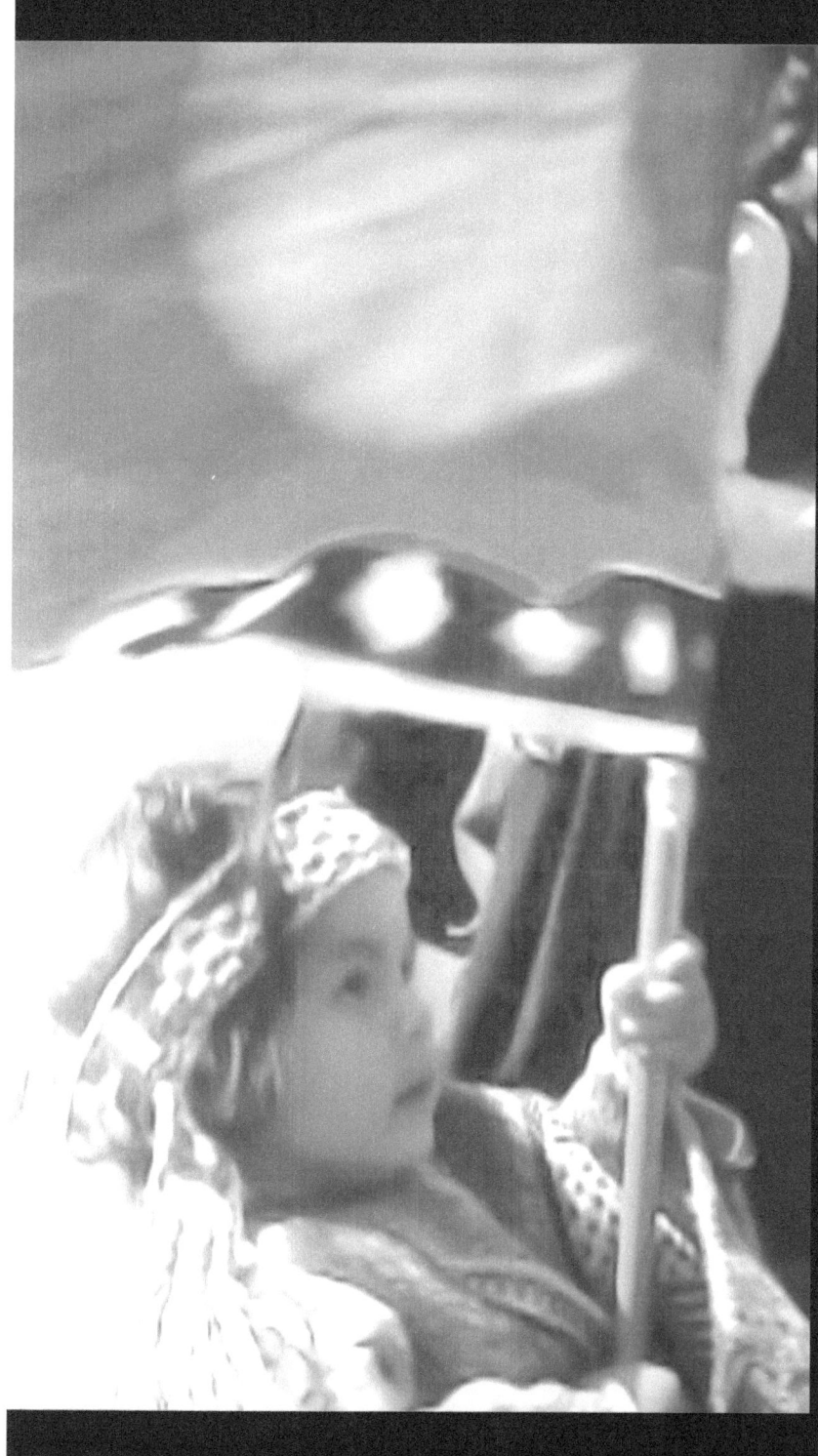

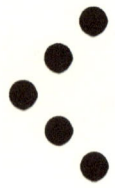

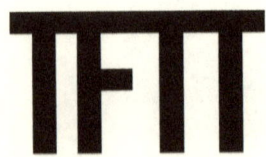

www.firethistime.com
jahdub.ghost.stories@gmail.com

www.ingramcontent.com/pod-product-compliance
Lightning Source LLC
Chambersburg PA
CBHW020421220526
45464CB00002B/510